T0304119

ROUTLEDGE LIBRARY EDITIONS:
INFLATION

Volume 3

INFLATION, GROWTH AND INTERNATIONAL FINANCE

INFLATION, GROWTH AND INTERNATIONAL FINANCE

ALEC CAIRNCROSS

Routledge
Taylor & Francis Group

LONDON AND NEW YORK

First published in 1975 by George Allen & Unwin Ltd

This edition first published in 2016
by Routledge
2 Park Square, Milton Park, Abingdon, Oxon OX14 4RN

and by Routledge
711 Third Avenue, New York, NY 10017

Routledge is an imprint of the Taylor & Francis Group, an informa business

© 1975 George Allen & Unwin Ltd

British Library Cataloguing in Publication Data
A catalogue record for this book is available from the British Library

ISBN: 978-1-138-65251-4 (Set)
ISBN: 978-1-315-62042-8 (Set) (ebk)
ISBN: 978-1-138-65308-5 (Volume 3) (hbk)
ISBN: 978-1-315-62380-1 (Volume 3) (ebk)

Publisher's Note
The publisher has gone to great lengths to ensure the quality of this reprint but points out that some imperfections in the original copies may be apparent.

Disclaimer
The publisher has made every effort to trace copyright holders and would welcome correspondence from those they have been unable to trace.

Inflation, Growth
and
International Finance

SIR ALEC CAIRNCROSS

London
George Allen & Unwin Ltd
Ruskin House   Museum Street

First published in 1975

ISBN 0 04 332063 5

Printed in Great Britain
in 10/11 point Times Monotype
by The Devonshire Press, Barton Road, Torquay

To the memory of
ELY DEVONS
1913–67

Contents

Contents

Introduction

Most of the papers included in this volume were intended to be heard or read by lay audiences, and deal with matters of public importance such as inflation and economic growth. The others, whatever the audience to which they were directed, should be within the understanding of the intelligent layman, and also bear on major issues of economic policy: the forces governing the rate of technical change and the power of governments to influence it; the case for and against floating exchange rates; and the likely future of controls over international capital movements. I have thought it worth while to bring these papers together because few of them are readily available either to the layman or to the professional economist.

The first of them, the only presidential address by a professional economist ever delivered to the British Association for the Advancement of Science, is one of the least accessible.[1] This paper, 'Government and Innovation,' harks back to a theme developed in an important pre-election speech by Harold Wilson in January 1964 when he, too, was addressing an audience in Swansea. This theme is the contribution that science could make to the solution of Britain's economic problems and how governments could take advantage of new scientific discoveries. Mr Wilson's handling of this theme sent a chill down my spine: he expressed a naive belief in science as the means of escape from Britain's economic difficulties that may have impressed the electorate but seemed to me dangerous nonsense and led, in my judgement, to an intensification of these difficulties. When invited to address an assembly of leading scientists in Swansea, I decided to use the opportunity to make plain the limitations of government on the one hand and science on the other in accelerating technical change.

Nobody seemed very interested. Scientists feel under attack from so many sides that they are largely indifferent to what sounds to many of them like yet another attack; in any event they usually have no great wish now to be on the growth bandwagon. Economists having caught on to R. and D. nearly a generation late, give it an exaggerated importance in economic development and go on confusing science and technology. The public, although not above whooping on the

---

[1] Like my presidential address to Section F two years previously it was not reprinted in the *Economic Journal* but it is included in the volume of papers read to Section F in 1971, *Uses of Economics* (ed. G. D. N. Worswick).

Government to put everything right, is increasingly sceptical of the power of governments to avoid making a mess of whatever they set out to do.

The issues discussed in the first paper remain of outstanding importance in a world of rapid change and ought to be the subject of active debate. Even if the question were put in terms of slowing down or arresting rather than accelerating technical change and industrial innovation, it would still be necessary to form a view of the potentialities of governmental action.

The second paper, 'Reflections on Technological Change, was delivered as a presidential address to the Scottish Economic Society. It takes it for granted, as I have done for many years, that neo-classical economic theory, although purporting to deal with technical change, does so only in a rather formal way and provides little or no insight into the problems of generation and diffusion that are central to any worth-while theory of economic growth.

The vast literature on production functions is largely irrelevant to such a theory. It is not the growth of resources or a change in their relative abundance that dominates economic development but the intensity and efficiency with which resources are used, including all that goes to the opening up of new uses: the exploitation of new markets, better management, technical change. In Ricardo's day it may have been sensible to concentrate on factor proportions because of the inelasticity of land in comparison with labour and capital. Pressure on natural resources remains an abiding problem. But if our concern is with growth, not the limits to growth, and with manufacturing and trade in manufactures, it is the process of innovation that must provide the starting-point for analysis. This is not a process that is made appreciably more intelligible by geometry (or even perhaps by algebra) since it is essentially discontinuous and largely unpredictable. It is no accident that some of the most determined efforts to throw light on the process have come from economic historians.

There is of course a great deal more to be said about the way in which different elements in the generation and diffusion of technical change interact. In particular, the interconnection between scale of production and technical change seems to me to have been insufficiently studied. This is true both of origination and of subsequent spread. Sometimes the fruits of technical change are easily detached from their industrial environment, and transplanted with limited effort and investment; sometimes no transfer can take place except in a block of interrelated practices and facilities. But to do justice to the role of scale and market expansion, far less construct a model of all the variables, would take us far beyond the comparatively slight piece reproduced here.

In the third paper, on 'Economic Growth in Britain', the discussion broadens out. There is a very large technical literature on economic growth, both in industrial and pre-industrial countries, but remarkably few expositions for the benefit of the layman of the thinking of professional economists on the key elements in economic growth. This paper is intended to indicate the directions in which one might begin looking (which is, after all, the main purpose of theoretical analysis). Too much emphasis has been placed in the past on capital accumulation and this continues in the politicians' constant admonition to British industry to increase investment. While investment is obviously necessary in order to keep pace with market expansion, it is not at all obvious that increased capital intensity is an important source of rising productivity. When one allows generously for the contribution from increased capital intensity there is a large unexplained residual in the recorded rate of increase in output per head[1].

The most elaborate attempt to provide an explanation of this residual is that of Denison[2]. After analysing the changes over time in factor inputs, including employment, working hours, capital stock, etc., he finds what he calls 'advances in knowledge and (sources of growth) not elsewhere classified' much the most important element in the growth of output per unit of input. But 'advances in knowledge' is a synonym for 'unexplained' or 'residual, in the absence of further knowledge'. The simple fact is that while we can catalogue the sources of economic growth we are only at the beginning of a sustained attempt to impute to each source its contribution to the observed rate of growth (in productivity or output per unit of input)[3].

In the next two papers the interest shifts to inflation, its causes and

[1] I think I can claim to have been the first to draw attention to this residual (although I did not use the term itself) in a paper in 1953 on 'The Role of Capital in Economic Development' which is reprinted in my *Factors in Economic Development* (Allen & Unwin, 1962).

[2] Edward F. Denison, *Why Growth Rates Differ* (Brookings Institution, 1967; Allen & Unwin, 1968) and *Accounting for United States Economic Growth 1929–69* (Brookings Institution, 1974).

[3] If what Denison attributes to 'education' is included with 'advances in knowledge' for the period 1929–57, then of an increase in output per unit of input of 1·74 per cent per annum, the residual becomes 1·20 or over two-thirds; and the only significant 'explanations' of rising productivity become 'economies of scale' (0·33 per cent) and 'improved resource allocation' (0·28) through a movement of labour from farming to other occupations.

remedies. Here, as with economic growth, we are faced with a problem that cannot sensibly be discussed within the limits of the variables on which economists normally concentrate. It may be true that if demand is sufficiently restricted, and unemployment correspondingly increased, collective bargaining will in time no longer operate to force up wages and prices, while other sources of inflation will prove unimportant. But restrictive policies can have other consequences that operate even more powerfully: governments may fall from power and entire societies be torn apart before inflation dies away. It is necessary, therefore, to weigh up the *total* consequences of the policies recommended and enquire whether less drastic policies combined with a little public education might not be more effective in the end. It is this reflection that has given birth to incomes policy.

In the British case, there are added complications: the vulnerability to shifts in the terms of trade with other countries; the decentralised structure of the labour unions; the sense of lagging behind the rest of Europe; the hankering after faster growth and mistaken use of expansionary policies to promote it. But the British record is no more inferior in the matter of inflation to that of its neighbours than is the record in other areas of economic policy. The trouble is that slower growth provides a smaller margin and less room for manoeuvre. At the end of 1974 the size of the external deficit had reduced this to vanishing point. Power to reduce the level of unemployment in the United Kingdom had ceased to be within the discretion of the government, however much it might pretend otherwise. Some retreat from full employment, possibly for a considerable period, was inescapable and some mitigation of the pace of inflation might result in course of time. But what role was left for incomes policy was by no means clear. It has been the habit of British governments, except in 1962–3, to ask for restraint in wages and prices when the pressure of demand makes it most difficult to exercise it and to make concessions in the process that leave nothing over for the time when they might help to make such policies work.

In the background of the next paper on floating rates of exchange is the fear that inflation might get out of hand through a vicious circle involving first domestic expansion and an adverse balance of payments, then a falling exchange rate, rising domestic prices, an acceleration in wage claims and a renewed fall in the exchange rate. It is a fear natural to a country with very large liquid liabilities to other countries and limited reserves; and still more to a country where 'the rich live on the poor and the poor live on imports'. The fear was rarely expressed in the sixties when the debate on fixed versus floating rates was at its height. But it has come to be expressed in more recent years with increasing frequency.

There is of course no possibility of maintaining stable rates of exchange in a highly inflationary world: it is hard enough in a non-inflationary world. But it still seems to me necessary to draw attention to some of the inconveniences and costs of floating rates, especially when literally *everybody* is floating, and to emphasise the reasons why, in normal times, governments (and central banks) like to see reasonable stability in exchange rates or, if possible, fixity. While I should not endorse the common view on the Continent that the freedom that comes with floating is illusory, since a fall in the external value of the currency will speedily be translated into a fall in its domestic value, there is now some tendency in Anglo-Saxon countries to exaggerate the flexibility in domestic economic policy that comes with freedom to let exchange rates float.

The case against floating tends to go with the case for control over international capital movements so that the last two papers go together, however inconsistent their conclusions may be thought. I have examined the case for long-term capital controls at more length elsewhere[1] but the paper included here is somewhat different in character and looks to the future rather than the past.

I am conscious of my many obligations to fellow-economists, often unacknowledged, in the preparation of these papers. It is difficult to do justice to the sources of one's intellectual capital even when one is fully aware of them; public addresses, which make footnotes impossible, discourage the attempt. But the reader is unlikely to imagine that the ideas expressed have taken shape in the void. They draw freely on the common pool to which a whole generation of economists have contributed; and it is only where I have been conscious of a specific debt that I have made reference to the source. A greater debt, dating back to 1940, is expressed in the dedication.

A.K.C.

November 1974

---

[1] *Control of Long-term International Capital Movements* (Brookings Institution 1972; Allen & Unwin, 1973).

Chapter 1

Government and Innovation

I

For many years it has been the practice of the British Association to call on a natural scientist, almost invariably a Fellow of the Royal Society, to deliver this address. No professional economist has ever done so before and no one with any claim to be regarded as a social scientist has done so since 1935 when Lord Stamp spoke on 'The Impact of Science upon Society'. An economist, elevated to such dizzy isolation, must find it hard to decide what to say to his colleagues in other disciplines. It would perhaps be legitimate, when so many non-economists have used this occasion for an address on economics, to reciprocate by looking at the activities of the natural scientists through the eyes of an economist. But with the caution natural to one who has spent nearly twenty years in the Civil Service, I have hedged a little and stopped half-way, choosing a subject half of which at least is home ground.

My subject is the role of the Government in innovation and I shall be using innovation in a limited sense to mean the generation and absorption of technological change. I shall not be talking about the advancement of science as such, dear though that subject may be to this Association. My concern will be less with science and what goes on in the laboratory than with technology and making things for the final consumer, individual or corporate. The question that I want to ask is essentially a political one: what can a government usefully do to accelerate technological development? I shall bring in science only to the extent that it is drawn upon by technologists and so affects economic activity. To this extent—but only to this extent— I shall be reviewing how the government of an individual country like Great Britain can harness the application of scientific knowledge to social and economic advancement.[2]

[1] Presidential Address delivered to the Swansea Meeting of the British Association on 1 September, 1971.

[2] I am indebted to Mr M. Fores for clarification of the distinction between science and technology. See, for example, his 'Price, Technology and the Paper Model' (*Technology and Culture*, October 1971). For another view of technology, linking it with invention and 'sub-invention', see Jacob Schmookler, *Invention and Economic Growth*, pp. 5–9.

These are familiar themes, on which, as on all great matters, there is nothing very new to be said. I do not stand before you as an innovator. The issues involved are of great practical importance to us all and it is better to debate them in this Association rather than, as commonly happens with questions to which no one knows the answer, on political platforms. Not that the Association has neglected them. As far back as 1952 it set up a Committee at the Belfast meeting 'to study the problems of speeding up in industry the application of the results of scientific research'. This led eventually to a series of important studies of technical progress by two distinguished economists, Professor Charles Carter, now Vice-Chancellor of the University of Lancaster, and Professor Bruce Williams, now Vice-Chancellor of the University of Sydney. Since then the Association has returned to the subject on a number of occasions and governments have taken it up with more enthusiasm than discernment.

II

Let me begin by asking why we should want technological innovation at all. Indeed some of you may wonder whether we do want it and whether it does more harm than good. I might reply with Bronowski that, on the grand scale of evolutionary history, technology has made man what he is so that 'to quarrel with technology is to quarrel with the nature of man'.[1] It was the unprecedented step 'from using rudimentary tools . . . to making them and keeping them for future use that . . . sent man off breakneck at a speed unmatched in three billion years of terrestrial life'.[2] In the more humdrum terms of economics it is natural to want technological innovation if it is on balance useful: if it adds to the wealth of the country or relieves poverty and hardship. The case for more rapid technological innovation broadly coincides with the case for faster economic growth. You may not find this case persuasive or you may think that, with increasing affluence, there are good grounds for a less wholehearted dedication to the pursuit of wealth. If so, I hope that you will bear with me if I do not turn aside to argue the pros and cons but pass them sternly by. I am going to assume that, rightly or wrongly, governments want faster growth and that it is this that kindles their interest in science and technology.

I do want to insist, however, that technological change has been the mainspring of economic and social progress over the past two

[1] J. Bronowski, 'Technology and Culture in Evolution,' *Cambridge Review*, 8 May, 1970, p. 141.
[2] Ibid.

centuries, and that it remains the chief source of our increasing affluence. Whatever may be said to pooh-pooh or deride economic growth—and economists are not behindhand in these flights—no one would want us to go back to the mode of living of 1770, still less to the lower standards to which present population would be reduced if we abandoned every improvement in technology since then.

Perhaps we should remind ourselves more often that income levels have risen fourfold here and in other industrial countries in less than a century and that the greatest beneficiaries have been the manual workers at the bottom of the social scale. It is not because we work harder or longer that we are better off than our forefathers: hours of work are much shorter and the physical effort involved is generally a great deal less. We are better off because of the enhancement of productivity that rapid technical change has made possible. It is mainly this that has produced the rise in the living standards of the mass of the population, hardly perceptible from year to year but adding up to a revolution in each successive generation. In spite of social disasters of all kinds—wars, revolutions, slumps—by which from time to time the improvement in income per head has been interrupted, this improvement now continues at an increasing pace which in no major industrial country is less than 2–3 per cent per annum—well above any previously sustained rate of advance. Even in Britain, where the low rate of growth is a matter of reproach, productivity is rising three times as fast as in the nineteenth century when we led the field.

It would be absurd to attribute the whole of this improvement to technological innovation. Something is due also to the expansion in world markets, the accumulation of capital, better education, new methods of business organisation and so on. But all of these take second place to advances in technology and some are themselves largely the fruit of those advances. There would have been little expansion in world trade, for example, without the steamship. More rapid capital accumulation would be to little purpose without a progressive improvement in new equipment. And so on.

If one looks back, it is the introduction of new products and new techniques that increasingly dominates the process of growth. Technical change, once discontinuous and erratic, is now sweeping us along and transforming our environment and style of life.

If this is what dominates the process of economic development, it is obviously of first-class importance to know to what extent more rapid technological innovation can itself be fostered by deliberate policy. Which of the different elements involved—and obviously there are quite a number—can the Government usefully influence? How should it set about influencing them? These are not questions to which a conclusive and unanimous answer is ever likely to be given: we are dealing with political attitudes as well as hard facts. Attitudes change from one generation to the next and so does the scope for government action. Some people are predisposed to believe that government action could accelerate economic progress while others are sceptical.

A hundred years ago the dominant philosophy was that governments should stand aside and not get in the way of individual effort to translate more skill and knowledge into a more efficient use of resources. The function of government was seen as one of maintaining a social and political framework within which technical change could occur rapidly, promoted by the spur of profit and the pressure of competition. The framework might be adjusted as technological and social factors interacted, creating new needs and fresh tensions, but innovation was left to take place sporadically within the private sector of the economy in response to commercial pressures and opportunities.

In these circumstances technological innovation in Britain and abroad owed little to government support in any form. It would be difficult to name any invention of importance in civilian life made by a government employee or at government expense in Britain before the Second World War. It is true that efforts were made in various countries and at various times to encourage new industries; but this rarely meant singling out some departure in technology for official support. One well-known exception was the prize offered by the British Government at the beginning of the eighteenth century for the development of an improved chronometer. The Government was also, by virtue of its spending power, in a position to assist the more rapid diffusion of technical improvements. An example of this was the use of mail subsidies to Cunard in the 1840s by the British Post Office which accelerated the introduction of passenger steamship service across the Atlantic. But in general the Government regarded patents as the appropriate way of encouraging the innovator and competition as the appropriate way of promoting rapid diffusion of the innovation.

To all this defence provided a major exception. From a very early period governments were interested in promoting inventive activity and accelerating changes in the design of weapons for defensive purposes. Where they were the buyers, they had a direct interest in seeing to it that the products offered to them were in advance of those available to potential enemies. This did not mean that governments were very successful in their efforts to improve weapons by additional expenditure. Indeed many of the more important developments took place almost in defiance of governments, as is apparent, for example, in the case of the Spitfire in the 1930s. But, successful or not, the objective of governments usually embraced the need to improve weapons technology long before any similar objectives were expressed in relation to private industry.

Over the past century defence has come to seem less the exception than the rule. Governments are now as anxious to see civil industry adopt the latest technology as they are to be up-to-date in the military sphere. What is much more to the point, they are far more deeply involved in what civil industry does and far less willing to assume that what it does from self-interest will produce the best results. Without quite nationalising so-called private industry they have semi-nationalised a great deal of it. They have accepted the role of managing the entire economy in the interests of full employment, economic growth, and other broad objectives of policy. In discharging this role they have greatly enlarged the public sector of the economy: in the United Kingdom, for example, public authorities employ one man in four and over 40 per cent of the national income passes through their hands. The State has thus acquired wider functions, wider powers and greater leverage on the economy.

For the first time technological innovation as a major source of economic growth has become an object of conscious government policy. This has coincided with two important developments with which I should like to deal at some length. The first is the growth of a widespread belief in the power of governments to use science for economic ends. The second is the growth of expenditure on research and development and of attempts to help private industry by government expenditure on technological innovation.

III

Popular faith in the economic potential of science is not hard to understand. It found forcible expression in Mr Wilson's speech in this very town seven years ago. Many people have argued that if governments can put a man on the moon or produce atomic bombs by mobilising the scientific and technical brainpower of the country they should be capable by a similar concentration of resources of eliminating human poverty and distress. It is often suggested that if it was right in wartime to build up teams of scientists and spend heavily on the development of new weapons of destruction it must be equally right to follow similar strategy for the purposes of peace. To those who think along those lines it hardly matters that the *British* Government has yet to launch a satellite successfully, much less put a man on the moon, or that there is a rather fundamental difference between a single consumer and a single project with a clearly defined objective and innumerable consumers wanting a multiplicity of things and exercising their preferences in unpredictable ways. Science is thought of as the modern Aladdin's lamp which, if rubbed the right way, can work miracles.

This belief in science—and I mean science rather than technology—has been given added intensity in Britain by the disappointment felt in the rate of economic growth over the past twenty years. Comparisons are drawn with countries that were in ruins only a few years ago and have now achieved higher levels of output per head than the United Kingdom without ceasing to chalk up a faster rate of growth from year to year. There is less recognition that the divergence between British and continental rates of growth is of long standing, extending back for almost a century, or that the British record since the war compares very favourably with that of earlier periods in which we now take pride. It is still widely felt that industry has fallen down on the job. What more natural than to turn to science in which Britain has an outstanding record and press the Government to let science come to the rescue of the economy.

If indeed science could do the trick the British Government would be well placed to take the action necessary. It is by far the largest employer of staff with a scientific training. If all government demands are added up, they absorb two out of three of those qualified scientists and technologists in Britain who work in industry or in government research establishments. About two-thirds of all expenditure on research and development is financed by the State and of this the amount spent on defence alone exceeds the total spent by (private) civil industry on research and development.

There are, of course, many people who would be sceptical of the ability of governments to make the right use of scientists and technologists. They would say that if the rate of growth has been disappointing, this is because governments try to do too much already. The last thing that governments are equipped to do is to promote industrial innovation. They can never spot the real winners because they are far too clumsy, ignorant and bureaucratic. Instead they are likely to go in for expensive prestige projects that tie up scarce design teams until another government comes in and scraps the whole affair. Do not let us be blinded by this talk of science, they might say, when nothing could be more unscientific than a government.

I have some sympathy with this view. I would not dispute that we should be on our guard against the tendency in modern life to call for government action whenever things are thought unsatisfactory. It is an illusion to suppose that governments can do everything or that government action is always for the best. They have their limitations like every other human agency and these limitations are most evident when we ask too much of them. If we want to encourage innovation we must face the possibility, to put it no higher, that there is very little that governments can do about it or at least that they would be well advised to find indirect rather than direct ways of operating on it. We must take governments as we find them, not as idealised, infallible do-gooders.

But we cannot shut our eyes to the powers and responsibilities that governments already possess. The greater the area of the economy which is owned or controlled by the Government, the greater, almost by definition, must be its role in technological development. To take the extreme case of a collectivist economy like the USSR where the whole of industry is owned by the Government, who else but the Government can apply scientific knowledge to industrial innovation? In a mixed economy like Britain, the Government's powers may be less extensive but it is in a strong position to influence almost every industry of any importance whether by providing a market for its output or by offering financial assistance for specific purposes or by abating taxation or by taking measures to regulate competition, limit prices, and so on. It is unthinkable that where the Government has such influence it should deliberately refrain from bringing it to bear on technological development and from seeking to increase industrial productivity by encouraging innovation.

But is it science that the Government should be seeking to make use of for this purpose? This is far from self-evident. What science yields is knowledge but knowledge by itself need not give rise to any improvement in the practical arts. This is obviously true, in the short run at least, of advances in pure science. But even in applied science much of the research that is undertaken may have no immediate application or, where it has, may be of no economic value.

Historically there is little to show that the process of innovation owed much directly, even if it owed a great deal indirectly, to advances in scientific knowledge. The key figures were the inventor and the businessman, who might be the same person, and might or might not be steeped in the relevant scientific literature. Inventions, whether patented or not, were dominated by the need to solve practical problems rather than by some recent scientific discovery. In a study of nearly 1000 important inventions undertaken by Professor Schmookler he found no single instance in the four American industries which he investigated—petroleum refining, paper making, railways and farming—in which a scientific discovery between 1800 and 1957 was cited as the factor initiating the invention. In almost all of them the stimulus was 'a technical problem or opportunity conceived largely in economic terms'.[1]

At the beginning of the nineteenth century it was France, not Britain, that led Europe in the sciences but it was Britain that was the acknowledged leader in technological innovation.[2] Until comparatively recently science remained very much in the background and technology although it drew on science, responded far more to market pressures. Up to the Second World War quite a sketchy knowledge of science was sufficient even in some of the science-based industries. In the days of subsonic flight, a recent study of the aircraft industry points out, 'it was possible to build an aeroplane. . . that would perform adequately if inefficiently without paying much attention to science'.[3] Whittle's invention of the jet engine was based on a cadet's knowledge of engine design.[4] Wankel's rotary piston engine was the work of a man with no university training.

You may think this exceptional but it is in fact far more typical of innovation than satellites and moon travel. New concepts and designs are by no means exclusively the work of university-trained scientists or even of university-trained engineers. In the 1950s half the patents taken out in the United States were issued to non-graduates. It is also an illusion to suppose that innovations originate almost entirely in large research and development departments. The trend may well be in that direction to judge from the rising proportion of patents that are taken out by companies rather than by individual inventors. But the individual inventor remains responsible for a surprising number of the major inventions of the twentieth century.[5] Although of diminishing importance in the newer industries where the links between science and technology tend to be closest, he continues to play an important part in industrial innovation. Whereas independent

[1] J. Schmookler, *Invention and Economic Growth*, p. 67.
[2] T. S. Kuhn, in *The Rate and Direction of Inventive Activity* (National Bureau of Economic Research, Princeton University Press, 1962), p. 453.
[3] D. Sawers and Ronald Miller, *The Technical Development of Modern Aviation*, p. 254.
[4] Ibid., p. 253.
[5] J. Jewkes, D. Sawers and R. Stillerman, *The Sources of Invention*.

inventors in the United States account for only 3 per cent of chemical and 9 per cent of electrical inventions covered by new patents, they account for no less than 88 per cent of mechanical inventions.[1]

New concepts have usually to be embodied in a working model and tested out in a pilot plant. But even then, nothing may come of them; about half the ideas reaching the stage of a working model are subsequently abandoned. The crucial decision is to embark on full-scale commercial production and it is usually at this stage that large amounts of capital are involved with the attendant risk of outright loss. Projects that have been fully tested up to this point will be looked at by businessmen from the same point of view as other investments bearing similar risks and without much regard to the element of new scientific knowledge embodied in them.

When we turn from the generation of technological change to its diffusion we have to think in international terms. Innovation in any one country does not rest on the base of invention in that country alone. It is an axiom that most inventions are made abroad. No country need limit itself to using its own inventions since it can licence or improve on inventions made elsewhere. Even if it is not so quick off the mark as enterprises in the country where the invention is made there is typically a period of many years—rarely less than ten—from the date of first commercial application to use by all the major firms in that country.[2] Since the rate of diffusion tends to be slow there is usually some opportunity, if other conditions are favourable, to catch up with the competitors or at least stay in business with them.

I should not wish to imply that diffusion is no more than replication of what has been done elsewhere. New machines and new processes, for example, have to be adapted to local circumstances including differences in relative costs, market opportunities and local attitudes. What takes place in the process of diffusion is a form of reinvention essentially similar to invention itself. The process calls for highly skilled staff that is capable of spotting what might be borrowed and improved upon and can insure that it is appropriate not only to local conditions at the time but to conditions as they change in the course of time.

It is a mistake, particularly if one is thinking in national terms, to put the emphasis on major inventions when these may well form only a limited part of the whole process of technological development,

[1] R. R. Nelson, M. J. Peck and E. D. Kalachek, *Technology, Economic Growth and Public Policy*, p. 58n.
[2] E. Mansfield, *Industrial Research and Technological Innovation*, p. 204.

while mini-invention—the gradual piecemeal improvement of existing processes and products that goes forward all the time—is easily
overlooked and is likely to add up to a much more significant
contribution to the total. No one invented the ship, the locomotive,
the motor car or the aeroplane. But all of them have undergone a
gradual and continuous evolution in design as one new concept after
another was subjugated to the needs of modern transport. What we
are discussing, therefore, is not a few conspicuous leaps of creative
imagination but the adaptation of new ideas to market requirements
and the bringing to bear on these ideas of technological competence
and commercial initiative and enterprise.

This part of my argument leads to three main propositions.

First of all those who put their faith in science as the means of our
economic salvation exaggerate the part played by the body of formu-
lated knowledge in the generation of technological change.
They underestimate the importance of unformulated knowledge:
of skill born of experience, of insight and perseverance in grappling
with the unforeseen, of inventiveness and imagination in design.
Scientific knowledge is only one ingredient in the solution of engineering problems and very often by no means the most important. It
goes without saying that the input of science has risen progressively in relation to other industrial inputs and this is reflected in the
increasing employment of scientists in modern industry. Scientists
may well be indispensable to industrial success; and industry may
make too little use of them or use them ineffectively. These are not
matters that I wish to dispute. What I do suggest is that if we want
more rapid technological innovation the contribution that science
can make may prove to be a limited one.

Secondly, while science follows its own logic, the problems to
which technology responds are set by market forces. It is the consumer, including the industrial consumer and public authorities
acting as buyers, who decides whether an innovation is really worth
while and it is his wants, disclosed or divined, responsive or unre-
sponsive to selling pressure, that stimulate the generation and still
more the diffusion of new technology. So it is consumer demand
rather than advances in scientific knowledge that gives innovation its
motive force.

Thirdly, consumer demand operates on innovation through
industrial management. It is the responsibility of management to
organise economic activity and decide when and how to introduce
new products and processes. If the Government wants faster innovation, therefore, it is industrial management that it must try to

influence. It may seek to do so in specific ways such as encouraging more expenditure on research and development. But it is likely to find that the chief need is to ensure that the management of individual businesses is enterprising and efficient and uses resources wisely in the face of opportunity and risk. Science adds to the range of resources on which management can draw and opens up fresh opportunities not unlike those offered by mineral deposits not yet exploited or not yet even located. The use of these opportunities, like the use of new mineral deposits, depends on the managerial assessment of risks and returns. Faster innovation means reducing the risks, raising the returns and improving the capabilities of management. But to say this is to say that innovation is like any other aspects of industrial efficiency: the prescription for greater efficiency and faster innovation is broadly speaking the same.

I V

This brings me to the second point of my argument. What are we to make of the growth of large-scale research and development and of the science-based industries that make use of it ? Does this not change the whole basis on which industry rests and put the relationship between government and industry on a quite different footing ? If the Government undertook more research and development on behalf of private industry in its own establishments or commissioned it from private firms, could this not be a major contribution to technological development ? Are we not in danger of falling behind other countries by neglecting these possibilities ?

There is no doubt of the vast scale on which research and development is now conducted. In the United States an expenditure of less than $600 million in 1940 had grown by 1966 to $22,600 million or from 0·6 per cent of GNP to over 3 per cent. The United States employs on R. and D. about 2·5 times as many scientists and engineers as Western Europe. NASA alone has a budget twice as big as the total amount that is spent on all research and development in the United Kingdom. Even if one looks exclusively at expenditure by civil industry, however financed, US expenditure is ten times as great as British and even higher in relation to any other industrial country. A single American company, IBM spends as much on R. and D. alone as the British computer industry spends on producing computers.

Such a disproportion has alarmed many commentators who see in it the portent of an increasing domination of world markets in the research-intensive industries by the United States and a corresponding subordination of European industry unless it responds as a single technological community.[1]

But has the emergence of R. and D. on the grand scale really transformed the situation? I think that the answer is no, or at least not yet.

First of all, whether massive investment in R. and D. is crucial to industrial success or not, there is simply no possibility of matching the American level of expenditure. The amounts involved are far too large for this. It is not as if the scale of research and development in Britain were out of keeping with other features of the British economy or low in comparison with continental countries. The margin of ten to one by which American R. and D. exceeds British corresponds to the relative dimensions of the two economies as measured, for example, by GNP. If the outlay on research and development is smaller in Britain, so is the size of the market, the average scale of production, length of run, volume of investment, and so on. Unless these things are changed too, a big increase in R. and D. might prove indigestible within the limits of British business conditions.

The growth of R. and D., moreover, is highly concentrated in a small group of industries. In the United States nearly two-thirds of the total expenditure comes from federal funds and is directed largely towards defence and space projects. Two manufacturing industries—aircraft and missiles and electrical equipment and communication—employ well over half the scientists and engineers engaged in industrial R. and D. and four other industries—chemicals, machinery, motor vehicles and instruments—account for most of the rest. Only about 5 per cent of the total expenditure represents applied research out of their own funds by firms in industries other than aircraft, missiles and electrical equipment and communication.[2] Very little R. and D. is undertaken outside manufacturing industry. The figures for Britain are not very different.

Experience in industries where success seems to have been on the side of the big research and development departments should not blind us to the fact that there is nothing inevitable about this success. Taking industry as a whole, the evidence suggests that there is no inherent advantage in size and no inevitable tendency towards an increasing preponderance of larger firms over smaller, even if the average firm is getting bigger all the time. The rate of innovation, industry by industry, does not appear to be conspicuously faster in the larger firms. There is a good deal of evidence that the pioneers

[1] See, for example, Christopher Layton, *European Advanced Technology*.
[2] Jewkes, Sawers and Stillerman, op. cit., p. 196.

are not the biggest firms or those that are best equipped with research and development facilities. On the contrary, it is quite common when a new industry takes shape for the smaller firms to make the running, growing into big firms as the industry grows.

Nor should we assume that innovation takes place only within the research-intensive industries; far from it. It may take the form of adaptation to new equipment, materials and processes developed elsewhere. The most striking development in textiles may be the use of synthetic fibres which the textile industry did not develop; in packing, the use of polythene and polystyrene; in various service industries, the use of computers. The more this is so, the less does the competitive position of British industry rest on its success in the research-intensive industries.

There is certainly no correlation between a country's expenditure on R. and D. and its rate of economic growth. The level of productivity in America may be higher than here (and for that matter in a lot of other industrial countries), but it is not rising faster than here. On the other hand, Japan, which spends only half as much on R. and D. as Britain, has experienced a fantastically more rapid improvement in productivity. The rate of economic growth is not governed by the relative importance of research-based industries although the time may come when a country's progress could be hampered through lack of adequate economic potential in those industries.

As the example of Japan shows, it is possible to supplement domestic expenditure on R. and D. by making use of imported technology. What costs money is not the kind of knowledge available in text books or in learned journals but industrial know-how which comes from heavy development expenditure and tends to be a closely guarded secret—often not even patented for fear of putting competitors on the track. This know-how can nearly always be tapped by production under licence. While the disadvantages of licensing go well beyond the expense incurred, the benefits may be seriously underestimated. They include the power to start further along the line and save time in working out what is already known to competitors; the power to select from among the fruits of development elsewhere what seems best adapted to local circumstances; and the power to concentrate a limited staff on adaptation and improvements that would not otherwise have been incorporated. In short, licensing does not dispense a business from spending heavily on development but does enable it to spend with more hope of keeping up-to-date, and in research-intensive industries this is vital.

The alternative is to allow US subsidiary companies to establish themselves in Britain and introduce US innovations directly. This is, on the whole, the policy pursued so far. It tends to be viewed uneasily because of the dependence on foreign capital that is involved and the consequent surrender of control. But if British industry lags behind and foreign innovations are denied entry through subsidiary companies, they enter in another way through imports and this also amounts to surrender of control. It is the failure to innovate successfully that represents the true dependence on foreign capital whatever shape the dependence takes.

Experience to date bears out the conclusion that it is not easy for a government to speed up technological innovation by encouraging R. and D. It may begin by exhorting industrial management (and I include the nationalised industries and other public bodies in this) to spend more on R. and D. than they would if left to themselves. This by itself is not likely to be very effective unless it goes on to make more R. and D. worth while by subsidising it, or making grants (for example, to research associations), or offering generous tax treatment.

How far it should go must be a matter of judgement and circumstances. Industry probably underinvests in R. and D. because it does not appropriate all the benefits to set against its costs. Part of the gains from innovation leak away in lower prices to the consumer, higher wages to the worker and higher taxes to the Government. This alone would justify some financial support for R. and D. on a non-selective footing. I also see quite a strong case for the kind of joint venture in which NRDC now engages and for acquiescing in a net loss on the money advanced if it helps to quicken the pace of innovation.

Financial support may also be claimed because of the sheer size of the outlay required. No commercial enterprise in Europe could face unaided the cost of developing the Concorde. Only a government could afford to run such a risk. It is safe to say that even in the United States no single enterprise would meet out of its own resources the whole cost of developing a supersonic aircraft. But this is (fortunately) a rare example. Other development expenditures involve less of a plunge or the minimum scale is not such as to rule out commercial development, often by quite a small firm.[1]

R. and D. carried on in government establishments on behalf of

[1] 'Despite some well-known exceptions like nylon, the magnitude of R. and D. expenditures necessary to develop most innovations is not beyond the financial capacity of small and medium-sized firms.' D. G. Mueller and J. E. Tilton 'Research and Development Costs as a Barrier to Entry', *Canadian Journal of Economics*, February 1970, p. 373.

private industry raises issues of a different kind: issues of industrial organisation. Some of this R. and D. can be justified on ordinary economic grounds as a form of useful specialisation. As a rule, however, there is a great deal to be said for leaving it to industry to carry out its own R. and D. It is always hard to improve efficiency from outside: and efficiency in innovating is no exception. The same logic that suggests a decentralisation of production units to meet consumer needs suggests a similar decentralisation of development in those units. Development has to be exposed to pressure from the ultimate consumer if its purpose is to serve the consumer. Even in war-time the success of Rolls Royce in engine development owed a good deal to the direct contact which they maintained with the squadrons using their engines in aerial combat.

V

Concentration on R. and D. is less helpful to innovation than concentration on industrial efficiency for true industrial efficiency must embrace the ability to innovate successfully. This still leaves an important role for government. There are many ways in which it can contribute to industrial efficiency, even from outside, and so encourage the more rapid diffusion of new technology towards which its strategy should be directed first and foremost. It alone can adapt the educational system to the needs of an industrial society undergoing rapid and continuous technological change. It can try to maintain competitive pressure and get rid of restrictive practices, particularly those that stand in the way of innovation. It can take action to reduce uncertainty, stimulate investment and improve the level of management. I do not propose to discuss such action in detail since it has often been described and has in particular been amply covered by Carter and Williams. I will confine myself to three brief considerations.

First of all, the rate of diffusion obviously depends on the speed with which new equipment can be constructed and brought into use. It is one thing to defer judgement before embarking on an innovation but quite another to be handicapped by delays that eat into profits and postpone the next stage in the process. It seems to me that these delays have been one of the chronic weaknesses of British industry throughout the post-war period and that getting things done more quickly should take high priority as an objective of policy.

Diffusion also depends heavily on education and ease of communication, two interrelated factors within the scope of government action. Let me take them in turn.

The more scientific knowledge enters into technological change, the more important is adequate provision for education in science. But because of the prestige attaching to research, and to science as opposed to technology, it is no use thinking that all that is required is an increase in the numbers and influence of trained scientists. It could be positively injurious to economic development to concentrate on educating as scientists a higher proportion of the top talent of the country. For this might mean insulating them from industrial and commercial problems and encouraging them to apply themselves to these fascinating conundrums in which pure theory is so rich.

If we confine ourselves to technologists (including those scientists who become technologists) what is needed is not so much more technologists as better technologists and better training for them. There is too low a proportion of graduate technologists in British industry by comparison with other countries and too few of the ablest children opt for a training in technology.

This is not just a matter of the availability of staff for research and development. Innovation concerns the whole of industry from management to manual worker and from laboratory to final consumer. The smooth planning of an innovation into production and its subsequent presentation to customers at the right time and in the right form is bound to be greatly assisted by an adequate technological background in the design, production control and marketing departments. If British industry underinvests it is perhaps in this direction that underinvestment is most marked. This in turn may be because too few men of the necessary ability and training are available to fulfil these responsibilities.

Next, ease of communication. There is general agreement that a new technology is spread mainly through the movement of ideas men from one application to another, often in a quite different field. The circulation of ideas on paper is a less effective means of communication. There are many ways in which greater mobility would be helpful: above all we stand in need of greater movement between industry, government and academic life. Such movement is just as important at a low level as among those with an established reputation.

One particular form of circulation that might be more fully developed is that between the science and technology departments of the universities and polytechnics and industrial establishments. These contacts could be doubly valuable in showing academic staff the range of problems that would have wide commercial application and in allowing industry to benefit from new ideas. New scientific and technical knowledge is not always communicated with most advantage at board level and the value of casual advice given by word of mouth without careful study is often dubious. What is needed is far more of the kind of systematic contact lower down between professional scientists in industry and academic life that is typical of the best American practice.

VI

Looking at government policy towards innovation in Britain since the war I am tempted to argue, provocatively and dogmatically, that the problem was misconceived, the strategy mistaken, the tactics unsatisfactory and yet that none of this made much difference since the pace was set by an unfavourable social climate over which the Government had little control.

First of all, the problem. Post-war discussion was dominated by what were thought to be the achievements of science in wartime. In fact these achievements were in large measure the achievements of scientists rather than of science and, what is more, scientists acting as technologists, that is, helping to produce military hardware. The necessary scientific knowledge was largely available before the war; it was the engineering knowhow that had to be created. Cost, which interests the civilian consumer a good deal, was a secondary consideration: the development of the atomic bomb, for example, cost about $1,500 million and the outcome was uncertain until the first bomb was successfully exploded. Governments tended to draw the conclusion that heavier expenditure on science would yield a dividend in GNP and their emphasis on science increased as time went on. But the basic weakness lay in engineering: in the lack of appreciation in British industry of the value of outstanding design engineers and the simultaneous lack of interest in the schools in an engineering career.

Next, development strategy. It seems to me a serious error in strategy for the United Kingdom to have put so much effort into the research-intensive industries in the post-war period. Unlike some of our industrial competitors we measured ourselves against the United States in just those products where large-scale research needs to be combined with a large and growing market and where in consequence we were at a disadvantage. In nuclear energy, aerospace, computers, and so on, our achievements may stand out in comparison with continental countries. But they have not enabled us to meet American competition with much success abroad or even, very often, in our own home market. It might have been wiser to have concentrated on less ambitious targets, adapting and improving on imported designs, squeezing into the interstices rather than trying to cover the whole range of market requirements, and spreading our limited scientific manpower more evenly over industry. Such a conclusion is suggested, not just by the experience of Germany and Japan which were denied the opportunity of following our example, but also of Sweden and the Netherlands which have been remarkably successful in limited sectors of high technology industry. Perhaps too, we should reflect, in the light of Italy's experience, on the need to put at least as much emphasis on good design as on scientific competence.

At the level of tactics I would draw attention to two connected problems. There was a tendency to overemphasise the generation of technological change as against its absorption: an anxiety to boast of *British* achievements in the development of nuclear energy, for example, when we might well have waited to come later into the race. At the same time, there was a tendency to exclude civil industry from participation in development work carried out by government agencies and yet look to industry to find commercial applications at a later stage for the fully developed project: again I am thinking primarily of nuclear energy. This does not look like a well-conceived division of labour between the central authorities and individual managements.

Finally, the social climate. The innovating manager in Britain has a hard time of it compared with other countries. He has to contend with government regulations that absorb his time, with restrictions imposed by his workers or by his competitors, with public apathy, with the slowness with which things get done. Innovation is a form of investment and when the economic and social climate is uncongenial to investment it is naturally discouraging to innovation too. If the whole community were dedicated to economic growth and all that it involves I should expect the rate of innovation to respond automatically and to sustain faster economic growth. But I cannot help suspecting that interest in growth is fainter than we pretend.

VII

Any modern government, concerned to achieve a faster rate of economic growth, will look with favour on technological innovation. But it would be unwise to form large expectations of what it might do by direct action to promote it. There is no obvious accord between government and innovation. The one stands for control, law, uniformity: the other for creativeness, nonconformity, uniqueness. In a sense innovation is a form of heresy, an expression of discontent with the established order of things: no easy object of official encouragement. 'Science' as a distinguished scientist once told me 'is a subversive activity that flourishes best when nobody is looking'. In some ways the same is true of innovation. It comes far more from below than above. It may respond to the promptings of governments but it depends much more on the whole ambience of economic activity: the predispositions and presuppositions of the public, which governmental acts in a democratic community tend to reflect. If the consumer and the worker want more innovation they will probably get it, just as they will get faster growth if this is the one thing above all others that they want. If they do not get it, it may be because they are half-hearted in wanting it and pay lip-service to ideas which they repudiate by their acts.

Chapter 2

Reflections on Technological Change[1]

I

The renewed interest in economic development since the war has brought back into the literature an emphasis on the importance of technological change that was sadly lacking before the war. Much of the discussion, in this country at any rate, still seems to be misconceived. Just as many economists in the 20s and early 30s tried to explain unemployment on assumptions that ruled out the possibility of unemployment so one still finds attempts to develop a theory of economic development that practically rules it out by abstracting from technological change. Even the analysis of technological change very often pays no regard to the facts about it but is cast in theoretical terms assigning an excessive importance to changes in factor proportions.

These strictures do not apply to the growing literature about invention and its impact on economic growth. Much of this literature is American and seems to be largely unfamiliar to British economists; but even in this country it is well over ten years since the work of Carter and Williams or the publication by Jewkes and others of *The Sources of Invention* and there has been a growing interest in the origination and diffusion of technological change.[2]

It is not my purpose to comment on this literature. But there are a number of points that emerge from it which seem to merit further discussion.

First of all, much of what has appeared deals with the factors governing the rate and direction of technological change, concentrating on the process of invention itself. It has been shown fairly conclusively by Schmookler[3] that there is no close and direct

[1] Presidential Address to the Scottish Economic Society, 23 March, 1971.

[2] C. F. Carter and B. R. Williams (1958), *Investment in Innovation*. Oxford University Press, Oxford.

J. Jewkes, D. Sawers and R. Stillerman (1958), *The Sources of Invention*, Macmillan, London.

[3] J. Schmookler (1966), *Invention and Economic Growth*. Harvard University Press, Cambridge.

connection between this and the growth of scientific knowledge although progress in scientific understanding is an important prerequisite of various forms of technological change, particularly in chemical, electrical and aeronautical applications. On the other hand, progress in science often follows rather than precedes technological development since invention can and does go on empirically without necessarily resting on a full understanding of the processes involved.

It has also been shown by Schmookler and others that invention responds to demand pressures either in the sense of market opportunities and prospects of profit or in the sense of obstacles to an enlargement of supply in the form of bottlenecks, breakdowns, etc.[1] Progress in science may reflect somewhat similar influences if one interprets demand pressures in terms of a growing fabric of knowledge.

This responsiveness of invention to economic forces is at first sight rather surprising especially if one has been brought up to treat invention as exogenous and unpredictable. But it is presumably no different from the responsiveness of natural resources to increased pressure of demand when this leads to more intensive efforts to discover fresh deposits or sources of supply. If we look at innovation as opposed to invention there is nothing surprising or mysterious about the influence of market forces. And it is of course innovation rather than invention that is critical in the growth of a national economy as distinct from the movement of the technological frontier over the world as a whole. If the fruits of invention become available after a fairly short interval to all countries irrespective of their contribution to the invention what matters in national economic development is the extent to which each country is able to profit from the invention and how rapidly it is diffused throughout the economy. This does not mean that we can completely overlook the factors governing invention; but it does mean that in explaining what is happening in any one country we are concerned far more with technological diffusion.

Now there is no reason to put this on a different footing from other economic forces affecting the behaviour of individual enterprises.[2] If

[1] A good illustration is provided by Schmookler's horseshoes case. He shows that the number of patents for improvements in horseshoes in the United States in the nineteenth century grew with the market and declined when the market began to decline.

[2] The modern treatment of invention comes very close to that of Adam Smith who treated it exactly like other elements in division of labour and hence as limited by the size of the market.

the relative prices of two materials change there is at once a need to consider substitution of cheaper for dearer materials and the process of substitution is likely to involve technological development in one form or another. If the growth in incomes opens up new market prospects, firms have to contemplate what would be involved in breaking into the new market with existing products. Here, too, changes in design and adaptations to market requirements might involve further development. The adaptation to change in either of these cases would be on all fours with the adaptation involved in introducing new equipment or a new process or manufacturing a product invented elsewhere.

Although it is right to put the emphasis on innovation rather than invention it is a mistake to draw too sharp a distinction between the two. Behind every innovation lies an act of invention (or, more commonly, a series of acts of invention) and the businessman engaged in innovation can rarely take over inventions ready-made and achieve a simple division of labour with technologists working for others. There must clearly always be an interaction between the inventor who is essentially a technologist and the innovator who is fundamentally a businessman.

Sometimes it is possible to distinguish between invention in the form of the emergence of a new concept, coupled perhaps with a working model, and innovation in the form of commercial exploitation of a concept after completion of various tests, gradual elimination of design defects, construction of a pilot plant, assessment of market prospects, and so on. At other times there is an almost continuous process, in which something is added progressively to an idea that differs little from earlier ideas but is pursued more relentlessly or in more favourable conditions or because some earlier obstacle such as defective material has ceased to exist as a result of other inventions. Even where one can draw a fairly clear line, the process of adapting a new invention to the circumstances of a local market is itself often an act of invention. We must not reserve the term 'invention' for those leaps forward in technology that strike the imagination and are singled out for mention in the history books. No one man invented the locomotive or the motor car although major contributions were made by celebrated inventors some of whom were also businessmen actively engaged in putting their invention to commercial use. The process of development was far more continuous; and this was true just as much of commercial experimentation as of technological.

So far as invention and innovation both respond to market forces in any given state of scientific knowledge, they can be regarded as adding to the elasticity of supply and at the same time lowering cost per unit of output. This double aspect of the matter is important in relation to what is said below on Professor Kaldor's work on industrial growth.

II

I turn next to the reconciliation of these rather elementary reflections with Professor Kaldor's recent work on the one hand and the wide disparity in rates of growth between countries on the other.[1] Professor Kaldor has shown that there seems to be a strong tendency for the rate of improvement in productivity in any one country to be sensitive to the rate of expansion in manufacturing output. This is a view which has been frequently advanced and just as frequently disputed.

I do not propose to go over the statistical evidence one way or the other but will for present purposes take it for granted that one can accept Professor Kaldor's various equations. When it comes to interpretation, however, there are at least three different reasons why output might show the response which he claims.

There is first of all a well-known formula (often referred to as Okun's Law) which predicts just such a movement in the short run in output in relation to employment because of changes in capacity utilisation. In most industrial countries changes in the pressure of demand tend to bring about larger swings in output than in employment; and if one could extend the short term relationship to longer periods, results would be obtained similar to those of Professor Kaldor.

Secondly, there are economies of scale which one would expect to show themselves in the long run and which have been thought in the past to go a long way towards explaining the higher level of productivity in the United States compared with the level in Western Europe. Some economies of scale would presumably continue to be enjoyed independently of technological change. But it is natural to suspect that where the market is larger the process of scaling up will bring further technological development into play. The methods of production in use in the United States would then reflect not only access to a larger market but also a different technology associated with that larger market.

[1] N. Kaldor, (1967). 'Causes of the Slow Rate of Economic Growth of the United Kingdom: An Inaugural Lecture'. Cambridge University Press, Cambridge. See also his 'The Irrelevance of Equilibrium Economics', *Economic Journal*, December 1972.

This provides a third possible explanation and is reinforced by Schmookler's emphasis on the responsiveness of technological change to market growth. This line of explanation is also in keeping with Professor Kaldor's discovery that it is only in manufacturing that his relationship holds good; for it might be argued that the process of invention and innovation is particularly conspicuous in manufacturing so that an expanding market for manufactures should be peculiarly liable to bring about an accompanying increase in productivity.

If one does not lay stress on the third rather than the second of these explanations it is difficult to reconcile Professor Kaldor's results with the obvious fact that over the centuries what transforms the standard of living and the level of productivity is technological development rather than economies of scale. What I have always found puzzling about Professor Kaldor's theory is that it should be designed to explain rates of economic growth over considerable periods of time and yet seem to leave completely out of account what, by general agreement, is plainly the most important factor in economic growth.

The third explanation runs in terms of an expanding market rather than a large market whereas the second explanation has to do with the size of the market rather than its rate of growth. Professor Kaldor's emphasis is also on the rate of expansion of the market. So I suspect that the validity of his relationship rests at least as much on an 'innovation' effect as on a 'scale' effect.

III

There is a second problem of reconciliation on which I should like to touch. If technological change exercises a decisive influence on industrial productivity and if the same technology is available to everyone, why do different countries grow at different rates? For that matter, how, without getting involved in a circular argument, would Professor Kaldor account for differences between countries? If the rate of expansion of the national market dominates the growth in productivity and if the growth in productivity explains why the national market is expanding at a given rate what leads to differences between countries in the first place?

We might of course argue in terms of lags. The country where invention takes place may be the country in which innovation proceeds most rapidly although this has not always been the experience of the United Kingdom. Would we expect the standard of living of the United Kingdom to catch up with that in the United States if technological change ceased? I should think not.

The lags which undoubtedly exist might also be coupled with cumulative effects and these certainly are real. If one country, like one firm, gets off to a good start with some industry it may build up an extremely strong position because other countries would find it difficult to introduce simultaneously all the technology and all the know-how required. Even this does not seem convincing when one looks at the way in which Japanese shipbuilding has come to dominate international markets in what, by any standard, has been an exceptionally short period of time.

One might argue also that newly emerging technology may be less well adapted to foreign countries because it naturally takes account of local market conditions and local factor prices and these may not apply elsewhere. There is undoubtedly substance in this. The equipment introduced in the United States may require too large a market to be worth introducing elsewhere or may be worthwhile only when labour costs are as high relatively to capital costs as in the United States.

If one thinks further along these lines one is driven to regard as a critical factor in economic growth the degree to which a country is equipped to seize on and adapt technological change originating abroad. It becomes a matter of organisation for growth just as the growth of individual firms rests on the creation of suitable organisation for that purpose. Together with organisation, of course, would have to go enthusiasm and receptiveness: the rate of diffusion is not just a matter of organisation but also of incentive and response.

But all this presupposes that economic growth is due exclusively to technological change. Of course this is not so. It may approximate to the truth if growth is taken to refer to productivity rather than GNP. But the market may expand because of an increase in available resources: natural resources, manpower or capital assets. Or these resources may be used more intensively because the pressure of demand is increased. Either source of market expansion would bring into play the mechanism discussed in the previous section.

Moreover, the market confronting the producers of any one country is not limited by national boundaries: it is dependent on trading relationships with other countries, access to foreign markets, tariffs, transport costs, and the competitive position of the country. So long as there are differences in accessibility and in cost levels between different countries, the rate of market expansion will differ from one country to another.

In addition the location of industry is not itself governed by the state of technology and there are always likely to be shifts in progress from high cost to low cost areas or from areas of lesser convenience to areas of greater convenience. The effect of these shifts is bound to be such as to depress the rate of market expansion in areas falling out of favour and to boost it in the favoured areas.

Again there is a parallel with the experience of individual firms and industries. Productivity rarely increases sharply in declining industries because they find it difficult to attract the kind of ability that is readily attracted to industries with better prospects.

In the light of these reflections one can account for the slower rate of growth in the United Kingdom in one of three ways. One can argue that resources are growing more slowly in Britain or that the scope for an increase in pressure on those resources is more limited. Or one may suggest that there is a shift, which has been going on over a very long period, from the perimeter of the Western European economy towards its centre, that this makes against the location of new and expanding industries in Britain and in favour of their location elsewhere, and that this reacts back on productivity in Britain not only directly by diminishing the share of the United Kingdom in the most advanced industries but indirectly by limiting the rate of expansion of the market confronting other industries.

A third explanation would emphasise the rate of diffusion of technological innovation and explain this in terms of defects in the organisation for adaptation to technological change or some lack of enthusiasm and incentive to exploit the opportunities opened up by technological change elsewhere.

Although the United Kingdom is a diminishing fraction of the total European economy I should be disinclined to lay too much weight on the first two of these explanations. The scale on which American business has invested in the United Kingdom is in itself an indication that this is still an attractive location for economic activity and that there are decided conveniences in producing here. On the other hand there are all too many symptoms of sluggishness in the British economy that seem to go back to an unnecessarily low rate of technological change and a multiplication of obstacles to it expressive of public attitudes that are less than enthusiastic. Everyone is aware that innovation lays golden eggs; but most people are anxious to claim the eggs without taking any trouble about feeding the goose.

IV

It is when we try to explain relative rates of diffusion that the existing literature is most inadequate. There is no accepted explanation of the rate of diffusion of technology between different parts of an economic system whether that system is the world economy as a whole or is some fragment of it within which change takes place at varying rates.

A given technological advance will yield different dividends in different countries. In some it may have no value at all because it takes for granted the existence of a large staff of skilled labour, suitable servicing facilities, etc. In others the return may be limited because firms are already employing the next best technology so that the net improvement from the introduction of the new invention would be small. But where there is a large technological gap, the immediate employment of the latest technology, if it happens to be within the capabilities of the country, could effect a very large net increase in output and productivity.

Moreover, once a country has passed a certain threshold of industrialisation it may be able to take advantage of modern technology without a great deal of research and development on the spot. It can, for instance, import equipment from abroad embodying the latest improvements. It can licence processes that have been developed elsewhere and will yield a bigger return at the lower level of costs in the country importing the technology. It can also turn to foreign constructional companies and ask them to put up factories on a turnkey basis so that the whole technological unit is imported at one go from abroad. On top of this, any resulting increase in real incomes will create an expanding market in which it is correspondingly easier for the innovator to launch his innovation so that the whole pace of technological progress will be quickened.

But this is obviously not the whole truth about the diffusion of technology. What has to move from one country to another is not just particular machines or particular processes or even the knowledge that can be written down in books. So far as machines and processes are concerned they have to be adapted to the local circumstances, including differences in relative prices, climatic conditions, etc.; and in the process what takes place is not mere replication but a form of reinvention essentially similar to invention itself. What is borrowed from abroad is subject to rapid obsolescence since technology does not stand still. There has therefore to be a staff on hand that is capable of building on what is borrowed, making sure that it is appropriate not only to the original conditions but to conditions as they change over time.

There are many difficulties standing in the way of successful adaptation.

For example:

a) Scale. If the local market is much smaller than that for which the original invention was devised it may be necessary to contrive some smaller scale unit; where this is feasible, there is likely to be some penalty in higher costs and where it is not, production will involve some waste of capacity. Smaller plant is likely to be less economic. Moreover the process of redesign will be attended with great uncertainty as to what will happen because a change in scale rarely involves only a single factor and the larger the number of factors involved the more difficult it is to forecast performance. If the scale of production is smaller this will involve simultaneous changes in other elements in the handling of the product or process such as marketing; and here too adaptation will be required or costs will be inflated.

b) Specification. Equipment used in one country may have to meet specifications different from those prescribed in another. This may be so because of legislative requirements or because of different local standards and usages. The equipment has to be brought into use alongside existing equipment which the new equipment does not make obsolete. The need to go on using two different types of equipment may set limits to the departure in specifications in new equipment that can be contemplated.

c) Materials. The materials available in one country may be of different qualities from those used elsewhere or there may be problems in procuring the necessary materials except at higher cost from abroad.

d) Labour. It can never be assumed that the dexterities of labour in one country are similar to those elsewhere nor that management has the same habits and attitudes. There may be a shortage of craft skills of particular types or scientists of particular disciplines or used to team work of the kind required or of managers with the necessary experience. There may be a reluctance to employ a particular type of labour or pay the going rate for it. There may be problems of getting new equipment to operate satisfactorily and with the right manning-ratio, especially if workers have been used to other equipment that is ostensibly similar.

e) Finance. Apart from the problem of working new equipment into a jigsaw of old equipment there may be financial difficulties in raising capital to take advantage of improvements in technique. Capital is more freely available in some countries than in others for new ventures involving a departure from current practice.

To a large extent diffusion of technology between countries is rather like diffusion of technology over an industry in which there are firms of very different types. A great deal depends on managerial factors. How well poised is the management to take advantage of technological improvements? How well informed and how receptive to such improvements? How much in touch with what is going on abroad and how willing to make use of foreigners in one way or another? And so on.

But it is not only management that is involved: there is also the market environment and the attitudes and values that it expresses. Are workers and consumers eager for development or are they unenthusiastic or downright antagonistic? Do workers prefer the kind of career—in engineering, in marketing, in finance—that will advance the pace of innovation and do these careers enjoy high status and rewards or is the work of innovation neither very attractive for its own sake nor given the esteem and pay that its economic importance would warrant? And what, if anything, can governments do to speed up the process of diffusion?

The more one reflects on technological diffusion the more apparent it is that it responds to much the same forces as govern economic efficiency. Diffusion will be most rapid where economic efficiency is most highly regarded by management, workers and consumers alike.

Chapter 3

Economic Growth in Britain[1]

It may seem natural—indeed inevitable—that economists should concern themselves with economic growth and development, a subject very much in everybody's mind since the Second World War. But if one looks back it is remarkable how little thought was given for well over a century to economic growth as opposed to such matters as tariffs, monopoly, taxation, imperialism, unemployment and financial crises. Economic growth was either taken for granted or submerged in more compelling issues such as tariff reform or trade depression. For a couple of generations before 1939 one hardly so much as heard the words 'economic growth'; and the very concept of more or less continuous expansion of the economy seemed novel and paradoxical when there were still widespread fears of a post-war slump and a renewal of the chronic and seemingly interminable unemployment of the inter-war years. Yet the country has been advancing for nearly a generation at a rate never before experienced and complaining that it is not nearly fast enough and falls well below what other countries are achieving.

In such a situation one might expect a flood of literature explaining why things have changed since before the war; why unemployment has been so consistently low and growth rates so consistently high all over the world; why the British record compares unfavourably with the record abroad; and what, if anything, can be done to accelerate economic growth in this country. There has, indeed, been a flood of literature; but some of it is not very readable and a great deal that is readable is superficial and unconvincing. I hesitate to add to the flood particularly as what I have to say may be thought to merit the epithets that I have just used. But I know of few subjects on which it would be more reasonable to turn to an economist for guidance or one better calculated to produce controversy and confusion in equal measure. Not that I aspire to settle the controversy or dispel the confusion. That is well beyond my powers. As with all major issues in economics it is only at election time that one is given simple and

[1] Based on the thirteenth Hugh Macmillan Memorial Lecture delivered on 23 March, 1971 and reprinted from the *Transactions of the Institute of Engineers and Shipbuilders in Scotland* by kind permission of that Institution.

conclusive answers and as most of us learn in due course the answers
then given become progressively less simple and less conclusive.

If there *were* simple answers to the main questions about economic
growth there would be no occasion for me to take up space repeat-
ing them to you because you would know them already. If the
questions could be answered only in terms of technical economics I
should hesitate to make them the subject of this article. It is because
the answers are not simple, because there is room for disagreement,
because economic growth cannot be explained exclusively in terms of
pure economics, that I think it worthwhile to pursue the subject.

The recent writings of professional economists on the subject
tend to fall into one or other of two categories. There are mathematical treatments in terms of growth models which economists
construct with great facility and which explain practically everything
except how growth comes about in the first place; and there are the
statistical treatments which explain all the things that are so obvious
as not to need explanation and leave a large unexplained residual to
remind us how little we really know. The models are usually impressive feats of mathematical conjuring; but, as with most conjuring,
the outcome is apt to be mystification rather than clarification and
problems of technique receive altogether disproportionate attention.
The models help us to understand what is needed to sustain steady
growth and hence what may slow it down or arrest it, but they are not
very useful—or so it seems to me—if what one wants to know is how
to make growth happen or how to make it happen faster. On the
other hand, the statistical approach to growth, while it may assign
so much influence to this factor or that (such as increased employment, better education, etc.) never seems to yield results that add up
to the observed rate of growth. One is still left asking what has been
missed out.

If the explanations of professional economists seem inadequate or
incomplete it is hardly surprising if the general public feels a little at
sea. There is no lack of popular doctrine in the Press, in Parliament,
and in pamphlet literature. The trouble is that the fashionable view
keeps changing and the spotlight is thrown on one all-encompassing
explanation after another. First a remedy is found for slow growth in
higher investment, then in more education, including management
education, then planning emerges as the secret of success, or restruc-
turing of industry, or disengagement, as the case may be. Then we are
told that the way to the promised land lies through the Common
Market. There was a time when all our troubles were put down to
stop-go; and for many years it has been an article of faith in Britain

that growth would be faster if only the balance of payments were healthier. The one thing that all these ideas have in common is the assumption that Britain's economic performance since the war has been poor and that this largely reflects errors of government policy.

But is this assumption warranted? Can we take for granted that more errors or more serious errors of economic policy have been made in Britain than elsewhere?

Anyone living in Britain may be excused for thinking that the country is in a perpetual state of economic crisis, that governments keep shifting from one crazy policy to another, and that this keeps the economy from growing as it should. But there is little relationship between the atmosphere of crisis that so often surrounds government policy and official pronouncements and the prosperity of the country. In France up to the late 1950s the atmosphere of crisis was far more pronounced than in Britain and distrust of government policy went far deeper. Yet between these years and the period up to 1961 when French economic policy was held up to our admiration, and French administrative methods (often borrowed from earlier British experience) were described in almost evangelical terms, no measurable change took place in statistical indices of French prosperity. Growth was just as fast in the 50s as in the 60s. All that happened was that France moved from an external deficit to an external surplus, both of them extremely small in relation to French national income and wealth.

I do not want to give the impression that a large and continuing deficit in the balance of payments is something that can be laughed off as of no importance, or that the external debts that we have contracted in the course of the past few years are an irrelevance. But there should be a more widespread recognition that the balance of payments is significant not for its own sake but largely because it may in due course provoke sharp reversals of government policy and make it impossible to sustain the import levels necessary for full employment at current living standards. In the same way, external debts, if unaccompanied by adequate holdings of international reserves, may throw a country into an undesirable degree of dependence on its foreign creditors and limit its freedom of action in framing domestic economic policy. Without seeking to minimise the significance of our chronic balance of payment difficulties ever since the war, I would remind you that any debts contracted by the United Kingdom up to 1973 fell well short of the addition made to our external assets (especially if the capital gains on those assets are counted in). Our difficulties have come from shortage of liquid external reserves rather than from spending more on imports than we were able to earn from our exports.

But if the balance of payments is not an adequate test of economic performance, what is? What in fact *is* economic growth? For some purposes what is meant is growth in total production=GNP or gross national production: this shows us how much more wealth is being produced from year to year. For other purposes GNP is not a good measure of economic growth as it reflects increases in wealth that may leave us no better off: increases due, for example, to immigration of workers from abroad, or a growing population of working age, or the borrowing of capital from other countries, or any other use of more input to get more output. What we really need is a measure of growing efficiency because in all but exceptional circumstances this is the only possible basis for a growing standard of living. In economics as in engineering, efficiency is measured by output per unit of input and this, in fact, is what economists mean by the familiar term 'productivity'. Economic growth is best measured in terms of the movement of productivity through time.

This is not quite the same thing as output per head since labour is not the only input, but for many purposes we can equate the two and regard either of them as very closely connected with the movement in the standard of living.

If this is what is meant by economic growth what does the statistical record show? It shows beyond doubt that the growth of GNP in Britain since the war has been distinctly better than in any pre-war period of comparable length. The average for the past twenty years works out at about 3 per cent per annum, whereas in the nineteenth century the average was about 2 per cent and half of this was a reflection of the growth in the working population. Other countries, however, have enjoyed much higher rates of growth since the war, ranging up to nearly 8 per cent in Germany in the 50s and between 9 and 10 per cent in Japan in the 60s.

When we turn to the stricter test of productivity we have to take into account transfers from sectors of the economy where productivity is low (such as agriculture) to sectors where it is normally high (as in industry). While these changes are very important in some countries there is very much less scope for them in others. It seems best, therefore, to make comparisons in terms of manufacturing alone. The record shows an increase in output per man-hour in manufacturing in Britain of about 50 per cent in the ten years 1958 to 1968 compared with 80 per cent in Western Germany, nearly 70 per cent in France and over 140 per cent in Japan. It is only in relation to the United States among industrial countries that there has been a slightly faster rate of growth and, of course, the level of productivity in the United States remains well above the level in the United Kingdom.

There has been some evidence of a slight acceleration of growth in recent years in Britain (as measured by output per man-hour in manufacturing). But there seems to have been a similar acceleration elsewhere so that the *relative* performance of British industry in the last ten years has not changed greatly in comparison with the preceding decade. In short, productivity in Britain, and with it the standard of living, is rising faster than before the war, or in the nineteenth century, faster than a decade ago and faster than in North America; but this remains a disappointing record. Is it the fault of the Government? Or does the explanation lie deeper than any of the things that come within the reach of economic policy? What if, for example, growth depends in the end on social attitudes and ambitions, on the wholeheartedness with which material gains are pursued and the approval which is given by the community to their pursuit? The environment within which governments operate has its own influence on the way in which the economic system works and at the same time it conditions the responses of governments: what they try to do and what they achieve. It is a mistake to treat the Government as a scapegoat when policy is not an exogenous variable.

It is only too easy to put the blame on the Government. Governments themselves make very large claims. If sheer political enthusiasm and conviction would do the trick we should have nothing to complain of in our rate of growth. But while it would be foolish to suggest that government policy has no influence on economic growth, the question is through what economic or other mechanisms can it successfully influence growth. It is here that the ordinary man tends to become dogmatic or vague or to get things out of perspective. On the Continent, for example, he may think that the establishment of the Common Market provides a sufficient explanation of rapid economic growth although the Common Market did not begin to take shape until current rates of growth had already continued for many years. In the same way, it is remarkable how often the simple deduction is drawn in this country that since members of the Common Market have enjoyed rapid growth, membership of the Common Market would mean equally rapid growth for any country joining it.

Again, one often finds tremendous importance attached to the type of economic system. But a quick look round the world shows that there is no obvious connection between the rate of growth and the particular economic system, form of government, or degree of involvement of government in industry. In the post-war period we have had a succession of foreign prototypes held up to us for admiration and imitation: first the United States; then, after 1960, France; most recently Japan; and at various times over the past generation, Russia and Germany. What do their economic systems have in common with one another? In the days when indicative planning was all the rage, it was on the way out in France and had little or no public support in Germany. But economic growth was just as fast in the one country as in the other. High rates of growth in France, Germany and Japan have continued throughout the post-war period whatever government policy was pursued. Moreover, the relatively slower rate in Britain is not a recent phenomenon: it was as characteristic before 1914 when no government had heard of economic growth or knew what was happening to productivity.

If one looks to the underlying economic factors at work for an explanation of economic growth there are four factors on which economists would be inclined to lay emphasis. Putting them in increasing order of the importance which I attach to them, they are pressure of demand, capital investment, market expansion, and technological development. I regard technological development as the most important source of economic growth in the modern world, market expansion as somewhat less important, capital investment as more symp omatic and consequential but also exercising some independent influence on growth, and pressure of demand as of very limited significance within the bounds of post-war experience. But since all four of these factors interact on one another and usually reinforce one another it is extremely difficult to speak with confidence of their independent influence on growth, particularly in the sense in which I am using the term, that is, growth in productivity.

Let me take each of these factors in turn, starting with pressure of demand. If there is a deficiency of demand, resources will be under-utilised or unemployed because there will be no market for the output which they could be used to produce. The level of utilisation or employment could be increased by allowing demand to grow so that it exerted greater pressure on available resources; and if this were done there would be a rise in GNP and an increase in productivity in the sense of output per head of the working population, including those who are out of a job. Probably, too, the increase in pressure would improve productivity in the narrower sense of output per man-hour; this usually happens as production moves up towards full capacity operation.

Something of this kind tends to happen in the early stages of industrialisation when agricultural labour that is not very fully employed is absorbed into industrial employment and industrial output expands without any perceptible loss of agricultural output. But the limiting factor in those circumstances is usually industrial capacity rather than demand. An increase in pressure is more likely to be the means of raising productivity in conditions of recovery from a slump—or perhaps a war. As demand rises towards the level consistent with full employment, job vacancies increase and more workers are drawn into employment while output expands correspondingly.

An increase in pressure, therefore, can bring about a once-and-for-all increase in the level of production so long as the economy is working below its economic potential. This is what happened when the slack in the British economy was removed before and during the war through the elimination of the heavy unemployment of pre-war years. But does a once-and-for-all increase of this kind carry with it a faster rate of growth from year to year? It may, and if the shift is a big one, it probably does. Growth is likely to be faster with full employment than when a quarter of the labour force remains idle. What is doubtful is whether the sustainable rate of growth is significantly different when a comparatively small increase in pressure or capacity utilisation takes place, particularly if it is already high. We simply do not know whether the economy will grow faster or slower if, say, unemployment remains around 2 per cent rather than around, say, 2·5 or 1·5 per cent.

Curiously enough this is a matter that has been little debated while controversy has raged for years on an allied but less interesting issue. I refer to the contention that fluctuations in pressure have a major effect on the rate of growth. You will probably recognise this proposition more readily if I call it the stop-go theory. As I understand it, the theory is (or used to be) that a perverse British Government has lain in wait until the economy began to expand and then— usually after a general election was safely over—has popped up like Punch with a package of measures to bang the economy hard and stop it altogether from expanding. Governments are said to behave like this because of the mysterious ways of the balance of payments, which get into deficit at just the wrong time. If governments would forget about the balance of payments and allow expansion to continue unimpeded, perhaps the economy would not only grow more steadily but a good deal more rapidly.

I had imagined that this theory was long dead; but it keeps cropping up in political memoirs, parliamentary speeches and the columns of financial writers. Governments are constantly being admonished to go for a policy of 'sustained economic growth' as if it were open to them by some simple set of enactments to raise the rate of economic growth. Nobody is obliging enough to explain how. Is there something that governments can do to improve output per man-hour in the average factory—something which remains a secret from the employers who stand to gain most from knowing? Or is the injunction little more than a semantic sleight of hand which exploits an ambiguity in the word 'growth' to make it seem to refer to growth in output when the recipe for action is cast in terms of demand and purchasing power? If we interpreted the magic words 'a policy of sustained economic growth' as meaning 'a policy of expanding demand indefinitely' we should be left in no doubt that the recipe was one for inflation rather than growth.

I am, of course, aware that the argument can be put in a more sophisticated form. Stop-go, the argument runs, was more than a failure to make use of available resources over part of the trade cycle. The real harm it did was to destroy the incentive to invest that results from a combination of sustained pressure on capacity and confidence that the momentum of market expansion will be maintained. In doing this it gravely injured the mechanism by which productivity is increased and growth accelerated. Even in this form, it seems to me intrinsically unlikely that if we could eliminate fluctuations in total purchasing power we would enjoy more than a limited response in faster growth. The fact that total demand was stable would not prevent wide swings in the market prospects of individual industries and, still more, individual firms. The uncertainties surrounding investment might be reduced but they would be by no means eliminated. Of the investment that materially enhances productivity, some might be delayed until expansion was resumed; but it is far from self-evident that the amount of such investment between one peak and the next would be much reduced.

It is possible that when a government takes steps to check expansion by operating on the level of demand there may be a corresponding check to the gradual improvement in productivity which lies at the root of economic growth. But there is nothing inevitable about this. In practice what we find is that when the growth of production is checked, productivity does suffer because of underutilisation of capacity, but the sacrifice in productivity is temporary and cyclical. It is not an enduring phenomenon but is reversed in the middle of the upswing when expansion is resumed. What happens to productivity in the short run is far less important than what happens to the underlying movement in productivity measured from one peak to the next. But there is no reliable way of measuring how far this suffers because of stop-go. Nothing in the statistical record can tell us what the trend in productivity would be if there were a continuous and steady expansion in output. The rate of economic growth might show an acceleration. But it might well be unchanged. It is quite conceivable that it might be worse.

When one looks at British economic performance against a long time horizon it becomes increasingly difficult to take seriously the idea that the margin between British economic growth and economic growth in Western Europe can be attributed to stop-go. The divergence goes back over the greater part of the last century, leaving aside the experience in wartime and in the years immediately after the two world wars. Moreover, it was, if anything, greater in the earlier post-war period. Additionally, it is important to recognise that by conventional measures post-war fluctuations in Britain have been of about the same amplitude on the average as in other countries, as Professor Tom Wilson has shown. The special feature of the British type of fluctuation has not been its violence but the literal alternation between periods of stop and go, the growth of industrial production since the mid-50s being concentrated in three comparatively short spurts. But the idea that Britain has been the only country in Europe to be afflicted by severe fluctuations does not bear examination. One need only think of the crisis in Italy in 1964 or the remarkable slump in Germany in 1966–7, or the events of the summer of 1968 in France to see that, on the contrary, fluctuations in Britain have been no more severe than those experienced abroad.

Now let me turn to capital accumulation and investment. Most of the writings about growth by nineteenth-century economists like Ricardo and Marx revolved around the question of capital accumulation. What they were analysing was essentially the process of industrialisation and what they had to say is not very relevant to Britain today. Nevertheless, we are still told that the secret of growth lies in capital accumulation, and that if only investment were higher, we should be in a stronger competitive position, our balance of payments would improve, and our rate of growth would benefit.

It is, of course, obvious that the more capital a country has the wealthier it is and the chances are that a wealthy country will be more productive than one that is poorer. On the other hand there are some kinds of capital which are essentially consumer goods, like houses, and have an importance in the standard of living quite distinct from any contribution that they may make to increased productivity. I doubt whether anyone imagines that by building more power stations and being equipped to produce more electricity we enhance our competitive position or add to our productivity. Usually what people have in mind when they start talking about additional capital investment is manufacturing investment, which is quite a small fraction of total investment.

But manufacturing investment is undertaken for a purpose and if we are interested in having more of it we have first to ask why it is no higher now. The main incentive to additional investment is an expansion of the market to be supplied. Manufacturing capital generally keeps pace remarkably closely with output whatever incentives are offered. Any attempt to force the pace by enlarging manufacturing capacity without increasing the level of demand is not likely to add very much to productivity. But this is precisely the issue that is in question. We want to know what will raise productivity not what will add to output.

It is perfectly true that the countries where capital investment is high are also countries where output has grown rapidly. But this tells us nothing about the direction of causation. Where output is growing rapidly the chances are that there will be pressure on capital equipment and a need to enlarge capacity. Hence there is no mystery about high investment in those countries: it is a simple necessity. On the other hand if output is not growing rapidly a limited scale of investment will be quite sufficient to allow capacity to keep pace. Indeed, if special steps are taken to make investment attractive by offering investment grants and in other ways the result may be more than a mild degree of over-capacity.

Admittedly this leaves unexplained the reasons for the growth in output and some people might feel that a higher level of investment makes its contribution to this. But there are many other ways of accounting for an increase in output per head; and I must emphasise that it is an increase in output *per head* that has to be explained and to which additional investment has to contribute. The figures for Britain do not leave one with the impression that investment has lagged behind output in the post-war period. So far as they go they show that the stock of manufacturing capital was rising appreciably faster than the level of manufacturing output from the earliest date (1954) at which it is possible to make a comparison between the two.

It is true that some investigators, notably the Brookings team who produced the best study of the British economy, have been inclined to draw attention to the comparatively low stock of capital in Britain compared with continental countries. But these comparisons usually allow very little for pre-war assets which, while not as up-to-date as they might be, are sufficiently serviceable to make their owners prefer to retain and maintain them rather than abandon them and install completely new buildings or equipment.

A shortage of industrial capital generally looks after itself. If capacity becomes tight the chances are that it is possible to earn a larger margin on the assets and apply the increase in profits to extending capacity. It seems to me far easier to cure a shortage of physical plant than a shortage of skilled labour or deficiencies in management and technique.

The third line of explanation of economic growth has a long history and runs in terms of expanding markets. It is this line of thought which associates free trade with prosperity and goes back to the doctrine of Adam Smith that the division of labour, or as we should say now specialisation, is limited by the size of the market. What Adam Smith might have argued in modern terms would be that the larger the scale of production the greater the scope for new and more efficient methods, taking advantage of a higher level of specialisation. This is not only a venerable theory of highly respectable parentage; it is also one of the very newest theories of growth propounded by Professor Kaldor.

Economists have given a lot of thought to what they call economies of scale, by which they mean increases in efficiency that become possible as output grows. For example, at the current level of consumption of electricity it makes sense to build power stations in Britain with a capacity of, say, 2,000 megawatts and install units of at least 500 megawatts where before the war it was normal to make use of 20 and 30 megawatt sets. The larger units have a much greater efficiency so that capital requirements per unit of output are lower now in real terms than they were in pre-war days.

This line of thought is obviously of great importance if we are trying to explain why productivity in, say, the United States is so much greater than productivity in Europe. It seems very likely that with her large market, methods of production can be developed in the United States that simply would not pay in the more limited markets of individual European countries. Hence if the Common Market genuinely proves to be a common market and the barriers between national markets are completely broken down, as has by no means happened so far, there should be a considerable enhancement of productivity within Western Europe. Similarly the access of the United Kingdom on favourable terms to Commonwealth markets before the war may have enlarged the scale of production in Britain and helped to keep down the level of costs.

An interesting example from the engineering point of view of what is involved in this explanation is provided by what came to be known as the 20 per cent rule. During the war Ted Wright, the well-known American engineer, developed a rule that if the output of a given type of aircraft was doubled the man-hours required per aircraft would be 20 per cent less than before. To put it in a different way, the labour input would rise from 100 to 160 when output rose from 100 to 200. Curiously enough this is exactly the relationship which emerges in relation to manufacturing output as a whole from some of the recent research done by Professor Kaldor. He maintains that if manufacturing output is doubled the labour input required will rise by only 60 per cent so that output per head will improve in the ratio of 200 to 160 or by 20 per cent.

This explanation offers very definite policy indications to a government anxious to accelerate growth. It ought clearly to be seeking to widen the market opportunities open to its own industries even if this means simultaneously opening its markets to the competition of similar products from abroad.

I should not want to deny the importance of economies of scale and hence of making markets more open. But I find it a little confusing that much the same phenomenon (of costs falling as output expands), with much the same parameters, should be explained in three logically distinct ways: in terms which associate increased efficiency with a continuing increase in the scale of production ('economies of scale'); in terms of increasing efficiency over time as a process is more thoroughly mastered ('the learning rule'); and in terms of increased capacity utilisation in the short term as the pressure of demand rises (Okun's Law). Why *all* of these should involve 20 per cent rules is highly mysterious. But I have found from long experience—and I am tempted to call it Cairncross' Law—that if you have to guess a percentage in a state of ignorance you are most likely to be right if you guess 20 per cent.

As an explanation of growth it does not seem to me enough to enunciate a rule of this kind. *If* manufacturing output expands there may be a bonus in increased productivity: but why should manufacturing output increase faster in one country than another? If the explanation is that because productivity is increasing faster the

country's competitive position is improving, then we may have got
the causation the wrong way round and in economics nothing is
easier. Even if this is not so, an increase in productivity, however
arising, makes a country better off and expands the market for
manufactures as well as other things. So one has not necessarily traced
the difference in the experience of different countries to its source by
underlining the association between rising production and rising
productivity.

Indeed it would be very extraordinary if one had done so. For it is
surely common sense that on any long view of economic growth the
major contribution has come from a rather different source: from the
superiority of modern technology over the technology of past generations. One aspect of this superiority may be in scale: in the difficulty
of employing modern methods of production without simultaneously
producing on a scale larger than was necessary with the methods
displaced. But this is certainly not the only feature of technological
advance. If technology stood still it is doubtful how far productivity
would continue to rise as the size of the market went on expanding.
On the other hand, if every advance in technology left the optimum
scale of production unaffected we might very well enjoy most of the
gains that now occur.

This brings me to the fourth and last mechanism by which productivity can be increased: the use of new and more advanced
methods of production. There is a sense in which all economic
growth reduces to this; but I am excluding, as already covered by the
second and third mechanisms, the use of more capital-intensive
methods of production or of larger and more efficient units of
equipment that are already known and available for use but which
it did not pay to introduce because capital was too expensive or the
market to be supplied too narrow.

There are many elements in technological innovation and
all of them are relevant if the issue to be considered is what can
be done to speed it up. But from the point of view of economic
growth what matters is the final stage at which new technological
knowledge is absorbed into use and proves its value by commercial
tests.

For this purpose it is not indispensable that a country should be
full of inventors or that there should be a large stock of research
scientists and engineers. Most of the inventions that we use in this
country were made abroad; and this is likely to be even more true
than it was in the past. Most of the breakthroughs in scientific
thinking are bound to be the work of foreigners. But the same thing

could be said in any other country and there is nothing to our dis-
credit in facts of this kind.

What does follow is that when we are thinking of technological
development as the mainspring of economic growth, we ought not to
imagine that the only way to make more rapid progress is to start at
the beginning. On the contrary, the best way to make rapid progress
is to take advantage of work done by other people. Tom Lehrer was
quite right when he encouraged us to:

> Let no one else's work evade your eyes
> and plagiarize, plagiarize, plagiarize

and no doubt we ought also to remember his advice:

> Only remember, please, always to call it research.

Since the war economists have paid a great deal more attention
to the way in which technological development occurs. If, in the long
run, this is what governs economic growth they cannot treat it as an
act of God because this would be tantamount to an admission that
they had no idea what to do about accelerating growth. They have
begun to ask themselves whether observation suggests what kind of
conditions are most propitious to rapid technological development
and what can be done by governments to encourage it.

This is a large subject which abounds in myths. All too often
technological innovation is confused with scientific research; and
science is represented as a kind of Sir Galahad that might be enlisted
in the rescue of the distressed maiden, British industry. But the fact is
that in practice there is little direct connection between individual
acts of invention and advances in scientific understanding, and still
less connection between these and the commercial application of
inventions. The essence of technological innovation is the translation
of an idea into something that not only works but works at a profit;
and this is a social and economic process in which the key figure is
the industrial manager, not the scientist, although the manager
would do well to be versed in science.

Another source of misunderstanding is the growth of expenditure
on research and development since the war. From a relatively
insignificant total in 1939 this increased to about £1,000m in 1969.
This enormous expansion has prompted many observers to think
that if enough were spent on research and development either in
government establishments or in grants to private firms this would
make a very large difference to the rate of economic growth for
which the Government could take credit.

In spite of the importance which I attach to technological innovation this seems to me a very doubtful proposition. Many large
firms here and abroad have had the same idea and found that it was
easier to spend heavily on research and development than to earn a
commercial return on the money. It is also not at all obvious why
governments should enjoy greater advantages over private firms in
respect of outlays on research and development than they do in
respect of other elements in business costs. In my view there are
better ways of encouraging innovation than by indiscriminate
attempts to boost research and development expenditures.

I would like now to turn back to some of the questions with which I
started and see what answers can be given in the light of this analysis.
The two questions which I propose to single out are how we can
account for the acceleration in economic growth throughout the
world since the war and why there has been a lag in Britain below
the rates recorded in other industrial countries.

I have already, by implication, rejected an explanation in terms of
the first two factors mentioned above. I do not exclude the possibility that full employment may have played an important part
but I am sceptical of the emphasis customarily placed on stop-go.
Equally I should not deny the importance of high industrial investment but think it more reasonable to treat this as a symptom of
economic growth rather than as the prime mover in it.

This means that I must try to find an explanation in terms of the
two remaining factors—expanding markets on the one hand and
technological development on the other. Such an explanation does
not seem implausible. The frontiers of knowledge are being pushed
back faster than ever before, whether at the level of scientific explanations of what goes on in the natural world or in terms of the pool of
technology on which industry can draw in devising more efficient
methods of production. The advances in science have been reinforced
by far more extensive and systematic exploration of applications of
scientific knowledge through research and development. On top of
this, thanks largely to full employment, business conditions are more
propitious to industrial innovation whether in the form of the adoption of new techniques or the more rapid diffusion of known techniques that have been tried out and found successful on a limited
scale.

The influence of full employment has been threefold. There has
been a once-and-for-all gain in productivity in consequence of
working up against the limits of economic potential instead of with a

large margin of unused capacity. At the same time, full employment has involved greater industrial prosperity and bigger profits out of which to finance research and development and the commercial application of the ideas yielded by research and development. Greater prosperity has meant, in turn, less mortality and delay in the application of these ideas because of the risk of loss in an unreceptive market. The fact that governments are committed to the maintenance of full employment provides an assurance that the market as a whole will keep to a continuous trend whatever the short-term fluctuations on the way.

This explanation is so general that it might seem to imply a universal acceleration and to be inconsistent with a lag in one industrial country behind the others and still more with a lag in a country where expenditure on research and development is high behind countries where it is substantially lower. But as I have pointed out the lag in Britain is not of recent origin and can be shown to be of long standing. The mere fact that Britain spends heavily on research and development does not guarantee more rapid technological innovation since other countries—Japan is an obvious example—may be more successful in exploiting foreign advances in technology. What counts is the rate of adoption of new techniques rather than of their origination.

Why then does Britain lag behind? There are a number of possible lines of explanation. For a time after the war it was possible to argue that other countries scored because they were starting from a lower level or had a large margin of unused capacity to draw upon or had a relatively backward industrial structure. Much of the industry on the Continent, for example, was carried on in small workshops, as was true also in Britain at the beginning of the century, and these were only replaced by factory production in the post-war period. A striking example of this relates to the cork industry of Epernay where a large number of workshops produced corks for champagne bottles up to the war and now a single factory is sufficient to meet the whole requirements of the market.

An explanation in these terms might have been convincing up to about 1960 but does not account for a continuing disparity in growth rates when productivity in Britain is demonstrably lower than in continental Europe. Some people would explain the difference in managerial terms; but the studies so far made hardly suggest that there is a great deal to choose between the competence of British and continental managements. Other explanations run in sociological terms: that we are more content with things as they are, more willing to tolerate inefficiency if it can be got rid of only at the expense of a first-class row, less anxious to wring the last penny out of business transactions and less ambitious to follow a career offering large financial rewards. There are also explanations in more narrowly economic terms: other countries have enjoyed more of a shift in the use of resources in favour of industry and this shift has brought with it an almost automatic rise in productivity.

Another explanation is that technological innovation is slow and unsatisfactory in Britain because there is something wrong with our technologists. It seems to me arguable that they are underrated, under-trained, under-employed and underpaid. Supply and demand conspire to make us less capable than other countries of innovating because we do not have the right men for the job. The bright young men from secondary schools who used to go to engineering works as draughtsmen now go to university and fight shy of engineering. If they think of an industrial career they have an eye on the manager's office or the research department and want to avoid the shop floor. Their interest in science is usually as producers rather than consumers. Design engineering, on which the rest depends, is left largely to the non-graduate whose scientific background is almost inevitably more limited. All this restricts the supply and quality of manpower available to originate or give effect to new technological concepts. At the same time the demand for design engineers is not such as to reflect itself in a chronic shortage coupled with high pay and professional standing. Industry is unwilling to pay here and now what might attract a higher calibre of men to the profession and seems very often to be oblivious to the difference that good design engineers might make to commercial success. The rate of innovation and growth remains disappointing because the input of new technology is too low.

All of these explanations have probably something to them. The difficulty is to judge how much importance to attach to each. My own disposition would be to stress the sluggishness of the British economy. We know that it is more sluggish than the economy of other countries: that all the main economic aggregates move up at a more gradual pace whether one takes GNP, productivity, exports, investment, consumption, or anything else. If there is this sluggishness, and if the driving force in economic development comes from the technological side, ought it not to imply that we are slower off the mark, more cautious or later in drawing from the pool of new technology than our competitors abroad?

Almost the only work that has been done to test whether this is so throws doubt on the fact. The National Institute for Economic and

Social Research has looked at the spread of new technology in different countries for a number of important innovations such as the float-glass process, the L.D. steel-making process, and so on. It finds the British record no worse than that of other countries. But I wonder whether they have asked the questions in the right way? Where there is a dramatic change in technique of which everyone is well aware, and where there is a large saving to be made by adopting it, there are good reasons for expecting one country to show the same alacrity in innovation as its neighbours (especially when one recognises how inappropriate it is to talk of alacrity in such a long-drawn-out process—for even major innovations take many years before they penetrate 25 per cent of the market). But it cannot be assumed that for the myriad of small improvements in industrial products and practice that make up the main stream of technological advance the same laws hold good as apply to the conspicuous leaps forward that seize the public imagination. It is perhaps because this flow of steady small improvements is comparatively sluggish in Britain that we lag behind.

At any rate it seems to me that it is more of a struggle in Britain to get new ideas adopted in industry or anywhere else. Workers stand ready to demand the full benefit of any improvements that are introduced without asking themselves what incentive is left to the company making the investment and running the risk. Or else they engage in a squabble about the piece-rate and manning ratio applicable to equipment already in use in other countries on more advantageous terms. Managers are too easily content to let things go on as they are. Then there are the consumers (including industrial consumers) who have to be persuaded to try things out and whose appetite for novelty tends to fall well below that of, say, American buyers. The government machine is large and relatively ponderous and makes itself felt more systematically (if unintentionally) as a drag on innovation than in some other countries where the public sector is just as big.

I recognise that Britain is by no means the most conservative country in Western Europe and that it would be difficult to account for the margin between the United Kingdom and, say, France in terms of some at least of the explanations that I have put forward. But if it is increasingly true that output per man-hour in French industry is appreciably higher than in Britain what is the explanation? Is it not that the French industrialist has rather more freedom of action when it comes to the introduction of new plant, re-allocation of duties among his workers, and so on? And that he feels more strongly than his opposite number in Britain the urge to innovate, which the Common Market in various ways has nourished? I would be the last to claim that I can account without ambiguity or hesitation for the difference between the British rate of economic growth and the rate in other countries. I should also be unwilling to put forward explanations to you that imply that the difference is inexorable and fixed whatever governments may do. What I hope is that more effort will be given to establishing the facts about our record in technological innovation and studying the ways in which that record might be improved.

Chapter 4

Inflation[1]

I

When I was a student at Cambridge over forty years ago Professor Pigou used to denounce the efforts of undergraduates to try to answer all the questions of the day simultaneously in a short essay. He regarded this as a disease and called it 'universe'. I am glad that he is not in the audience today or he would diagnose the same disorder. Indeed, he might be excused for identifying 'inflation' and 'universe', since I see that the *Oxford English Dictionary* defines inflation as 'undue expansion or enlargement . . . beyond proper limits' which is exactly what Pigou complained of in undergraduate thinking.

I plead guilty to choosing a subject far beyond the compass of a brief address. But in choosing to speak on inflation before so distinguished an audience I hope that I am responding to market demand and practising an economic virtue to which even Professor Pigou would have subscribed. I recognise that if I am not to weary you I must be selective in the aspects of inflation on which I touch, and will deal somewhat peremptorily with matters of technical complexity or professional controversy.

I shall start by making sure that there is no ambiguity over what we are discussing since inflation means different things to different people. I shall then ask what are the origins of inflation, reviewing factors on the side both of demand and of supply and international as well as domestic causes. I shall discuss how these various elements have combined, first to produce a continuous process of inflation in the post-war period, then to bring about the acceleration of recent years. Finally I shall turn from analysis to policy and consider what action can be taken to slow the process down again or, conceivably, bring it to a halt.

II

It is not surprising that the public should be in some confusion over what inflation is and what to do about it. In the history books inflation is represented as something that happens to countries that are

[1] George O'Brien Lecture, delivered at University College, Dublin on 24 May 1974.

66   *Inflation, Growth and International Finance*

badly governed, or subjected to debasement of the currency or at war or recovering from war. Inflation is understandable in Tudor England or Latin America or post-war Hungary. But why does it now go on all over the world? Are we all badly governed? And how long is it since there was a major war?

The confusion does not become any less if you consult the dictionary. This usually leaves you in doubt whether inflation is something that happens to the money supply or something that happens to prices. There may even be a hint that it has to do with purchasing power and money incomes. While the money supply, prices and incomes usually move together they are not by any stretch of imagination the same thing and any one of them may be the real source of trouble and account for the behaviour of the other two.

It is also confusing when the Government takes action that it describes as disinflationary although the obvious effect is to drive up prices. If it seeks to withdraw purchasing power by raising taxes on beer and tobacco, for example, it may argue that it is deflating demand while beyond question it is inflating prices. So it would seem to be possible to have deflation and inflation at the same time.

The case of oil prompts a similar reflection. Governments were blaming inflation on the sudden rise in international commodity prices as if they had no hand in it. Then the Arabs outdid everybody else by trebling the price of oil. Was this, as one might suppose, more inflationary than what went before? Well, no, we were told. It might jack up the level of prices in importing countries but it would operate in a highly *de*flationary way, like a decision by the Chancellor of the Exchequer to raise taxes by some colossal amount. Whatever the impact on prices, we might be landed in the worst depression since the 1930s.

What this brings out is that some people think of inflation in terms of the end result, which is a fall in the value of money, while others think of it in terms of what they take to be the causal forces at work, whether an expansion in the money supply or excess demand or an increase in costs or profit margins. In a sense the phenomenon to be explained is the tendency for prices to go on rising but the explanation has to have regard to different kinds of pressure producing this result and it is the pressure on which we need to concentrate our attention. Prices may rise for reasons unconnected with continuing pressure: a harvest failure, an increase in indirect taxation, a war scare, and so on. It is the continuing upward pressure, not the episodic once-for-all increase in the price level, that causes concern. This pressure could exist and cause alarm without any marked rise in prices under what used to be called 'suppressed inflation': a state of affairs in which a rise in the general level of prices is prevented or limited by various forms of government control, either directly over prices or indirectly through rationing, licensing, etc. But we can leave this out of account as of no immediate interest.

III

Why should prices go on rising? What is the pressure that causes inflation? Economists have put forward several different explanations some of which I shall outline briefly. They do not necessarily exclude one another and are better regarded as different elements in the situation making for inflation. At any given time one or other of these elements may predominate over the rest or bring the others into play.

First of all, there is the money supply. Traditionally, this is the villain of the piece whether one thinks of debasement of metallic currency or over-issue of paper notes or, in modern times, excess credit creation by the banks. The quantity theory of money on which I was brought up and which has a long pedigree fastens on the money supply as the determining factor in the behaviour of prices. This view has been elaborated with impressive dialectical skill and a supporting artillery of historical and mathematical fire-power by economists of great distinction such as Milton Friedman who have every right to hang out the banners of the day before yesterday's orthodoxy. They can point to the evident fact that an increase in the money supply does accompany inflation and usually keeps broadly in step with the rise in prices. But which is cause and which effect? It is only too easy in economics to get cause and effect the wrong way round or alternatively overlook the possibility that, so to speak, it is not the lightning that causes the thunder, or the thunder that causes the lightning but something else that causes both. It may be the rise in prices nowadays that accounts for the increase in the money supply or both alike may have their origin in something else.

Many economists would accept readily enough a long-run relationship between money and prices, with an increase in the money supply a pre-condition of any sustained rise in prices. But they would not regard this as constituting an explanation of the inflationary process without some account of the succession of events leading from monetary changes to price changes; and any such account makes it immediately obvious that it is mainly by influencing the flow of expenditure or demand that money bites on consumer prices.

It is common ground that, if money changes hands at a steady rate, an increase in the money supply and in the flow of expenditure must drive up either output or prices or both; and once output comes up against the limits of capacity, the increased flow of money is bound to spend itself in pushing up prices more or less proportionately. What distinguishes the monetarist school of thought is not just their emphasis on the pressure of demand and their relegation of supply factors to an altogether subordinate place. It is their insistence on the supreme importance of monetary elements in demand and the incompatibility between price stability and large injections of additional money into the system. They accept that there is bound to be a lag between additions to the money supply and changes in expenditure and output and a further lag before prices respond. But they argue that the public will not hold on to money it does not require at current levels of prices and incomes; and that the effort to pass it on will drive up the price of assets and inflate current spending until the extra money is absorbed into the system at an enhanced level of prices. The whole process they admit would be a protracted one. After reviewing the statistical evidence, they put the lag between additions to the money supply and a spurt in output at six months to a year and the subsequent lag before the rate of inflation accelerates at a further year—lags so long and difficult to demonstrate that they throw some doubt on the whole theory.

More important perhaps than the analysis are the policy prescriptions that follow from it. On the negative side these include a playing down of the importance of fiscal policy as such, on the grounds that the true significance of budget surpluses and deficits lies in their effects on the money supply; and a denial that incomes policy can be of any real value in containing inflation since in the end prices are bound to be governed by the money supply, so that attempts to control prices and incomes directly are misplaced. On the positive side, the monetarists do not make exaggerated claims for monetary policy but recommend a steady annual growth in the money supply in keeping with the growth from year to year in national income.

The majority of economists draw different conclusions from the historical experience of inflation and would not lay such exclusive emphasis on monetary factors. Changes in the pressure of demand are obviously important but account has also to be taken of inflationary elements on the side of supply arising out of collective bargaining in an economy accustomed to full employment. Such bargaining generates pressures of its own that may have to be explained in political terms and are certainly not governed exclusively by the state of the labour market. While in some circumstances inflation may be brought on by excess demand, there are other circumstances in which it may be the behaviour of wages (or some other element in cost) that starts off, or accelerates, the process.

This distinction between demand and cost inflation is sometimes challenged and an attempt made to reduce cost inflation to a by-product of demand inflation. It is argued that wage increases, and the cost increases to which they give rise, do no more than reflect a tightening of the labour market. If wage settlements are a simple function of the degree of labour shortage inflation can be attributed exclusively to the demand pressure setting off the rise in wage costs and prices. Those who take this view have scrutinised the historical record in order to correlate the behaviour of wages and prices with the contemporary pressure of demand as measured by the level of unemployment. They have then turned from history to geometry and drawn curves—named Phillips curves after the New Zealand economist who first conceived them—to measure the trade-off between price stability and unemployment, on the assumption that the figures can be construed as showing that such a trade-off is possible. But the assumption is not firmly based. It is quite true that money wages have risen faster in periods of low unemployment and slower in periods of high unemployment. How the fluctuations are to be interpreted, however, is open to dispute. All that we can say with any assurance is that in the course of the trade cycle wages shared in the cyclical swing and rose fastest in the boom when business prospects and confidence were at their peak. But this tells us very little about the influence of one level of unemployment compared with another. Wages usually go up faster as the labour market tightens whether the process of tightening starts from a high or a low level of unemployment.

Moreover, if instead of looking back at the rather dubious figures of a bygone age we watch what happens today on the shop floor it is clear enough that full employment has exerted a cumulative effect on the bargaining power of labour and that wage claims bear no close relationship to the prevailing scale of unemployment, although they *are* influenced by the amount of slack within the factory. It is not true that there is a simple and determinate relationship between wage settlements and unemployment. It is also not true that at some specific and ascertainable level of unemployment wage settlements would cease to generate inflation. Governments cannot trade a stated improvement in price stability for a fixed deterioration in employment levels; still less can they count on getting complete

price stability at some predetermined level of unemployment. That is
not how the labour market works. On the other hand, there is no
need to pretend that demand and cost inflation do not interact or
that excess demand does not aggravate wage inflation. Of course it
does. There *is* a level of unemployment below which inflation is
inescapable and likely to accelerate. Above this level inflation may
still continue but there is more hope of success in keeping it within
limits.

This way of looking at things directs our attention to a critical
zone in which, as demand increases, it presses more and more
strongly on capacity and begins to force up prices. Above one limit
to that zone, further increases in demand have a diminishing effect
on output and inevitably aggravate inflation. Below the other limit,
the impact of additional demand is confined almost entirely to the
level of output and the degree of capacity utilisation. At low levels of
output, prices may still be rising because wage-push continues to
operate. At high levels, the rise in costs and prices begins to accelerate
because of increased wage demands reinforced by the unusually
strong bargaining position enjoyed by workers and the trade unions
representing them.

Since the limiting factor in supply is usually manpower, the
critical zone in pressure on capacity can be expressed in terms of
rates of unemployment. Full capacity operation in an industrial
economy is much the same thing as full employment and when we
speak of the changing balance between supply and demand we are
usually thinking of the labour market. To a quantity theorist the
critical zone can be narrowed to a single rate, described rather
misleadingly as 'the natural rate of unemployment'. But to most
economists this is an oversimplification and we need to keep a more
open mind about the repercussions on costs of variations in the level
of activity in the vicinity of full employment.

In principle one may distinguish between the outcome of competitive influences on wages and a display of militancy resting on
monopolistic control over labour supply. But the practice of collective bargaining means that there always are and always will be
powerful monopolistic elements in the labour market. These elements
are visible not only in trade union negotiations at the national or
local level but also in negotiations at the place of work either on
earnings or on work rules resting on custom and practice. They are
reinforced by the scale and capital intensity of modern industry and
its increased vulnerability to the withdrawal of labour. The monopolistic forces at work operate so as to produce a ratchet-like effect

on wage settlements, making wages move erratically up and rarely if ever down. A breakthrough to higher earnings in one industry is soon transformed into a general increase across the board as differentials are first disturbed and then restored.

It is the presence of these monopolistic influences, which are not of course confined to the trade union side in wage bargaining, that has given rise to the efforts in many countries to deal with inflation by some form of incomes policy. Those who think of inflation in terms of union militancy are anxious either to curb the power of the unions or to secure union co-operation in the exercise of that power in order to reduce the pace of inflation. Those who think in terms of the money supply, on the other hand, regard efforts of this kind as likely either to degenerate into union-bashing or to result in fruitless negotiations in which neither side can hope to deliver the result expected of them.

It is worth elaborating this conflict of view. If exclusive reliance is put on monetary policy this will operate, and is intended to operate, by restricting demand: not just demand for goods but ultimately demand for labour. This can be represented as checking excess demand or as increasing unemployment according to taste. It is likely to do both. Whether this is a necessary price to pay depends upon one's assessment of the influences at work in the labour market: in particular, whether there is such a strong and unsatisfied demand for labour that this dictates the upward movement of wages or whether the unions are taking advantage of their strength to push up money wages and would not be deterred from doing so by some marginal slackening in economic activity. The appeal of the monetarist view is that it appears to side-step this dilemma by making the whole process a matter of banking policy and hence remote from such sensitive issues as the level of unemployment or the power of the unions. The weakness of the incomes policy approach is that it makes it impossible to deal with inflation without transforming collective bargaining from top to bottom either voluntarily or by statutory regulation.

So long as inflation was thought to be no more than the consequence of excess demand it could be dismissed as an error on the right side, obviously to be preferred to a deficiency of demand and the unemployment accompanying it. At that stage in the argument, fifteen years or so ago, economists were preoccupied by the problems of demand management (or subsequently of what was called rather derisorily 'fine tuning'). The issue was conceived of in terms of supplementing or withdrawing purchasing power in a context of stable expectations. The change in the value of money from year to year was treated as a somewhat accidental by-product of a system governed by other considerations; and so long as it remained almost within the limits of errors of estimation it could be regarded as publicly acceptable. The possibility that it might accelerate and get out of hand was rarely treated very seriously.

This permissive attitude was encouraged by a number of circumstances, some of them peculiar to the United Kingdom. It is nearly always true that when the pressure increases in a boom more output can be produced and at relatively low cost, especially in terms of the additional manpower required. It is therefore very tempting to disregard the inflationary consequences of demand pressure for the sake of the real gains in output that can be enjoyed. Of course, some of the pressure is translated into an excess of imports and this may drive the balance of payments into deficit. But while this may ultimately enforce a check to expansion it does so intermittently and at a later stage and so can be represented as a kind of intrusion which a strong and well-run government would firmly oppose.

One of the more obvious defence mechanisms of an overheated economy was thus dismissed as 'Stop-go' and attributed to government weakness. Coupled with this was the development of an expansionist ideology which saw in the release of additional purchasing power the secret not of inflation but of growth. Just when the pressure was beginning to mount dangerously, a combination of zeal for growth and confusion between short-term and long-term changes in productivity was apt to manifest itself and encourage government action to prolong or intensify the boom.

There is no reason to suppose that things would have been very different if the instruments of demand management had been primarily monetary rather than fiscal. Once the main aim of economic policy came to be full employment, the behaviour of prices took second or even third place. What was not clearly foreseen was what would happen to prices as everybody came to expect inflation. Once this expectation entered into the calculations of wage-earners—and indeed of all income earners—they took avoiding action which simply precipitated faster inflation. The trot threatened to become a canter and the canter a gallop. Inflation was no longer moderated by the illusion of stability. It is only in a world of limited horizons that these developments can be, and were, left out of the picture.

Each form of inflation carries with it its own illusion which helps to keep it alive. There is the so-called 'money illusion' that disposes those who are not yet fully alive to inflation to treat as a real gain any monetary improvement in their earnings. This enables demand to remain excessive in relation to output since the excess can be eliminated by an increase in price that was not foreseen when the bargains governing output were originally struck. Once the increase in price does become foreseen the bargains take it into account and if they did so successfully would effectively prevent the emergence of anything that could be described as excess demand. No one would be cheated and inflation would have lost its *raison d'être*.

Similarly, wage-settlements that in the aggregate cannot be satisfied in real terms may continue to be made in the belief that somebody, somewhere, will be squeezed. This is never entirely an illusion as every pensioner knows. But in general, wage claims continue to be pressed for the sake of illusory gains. The immediate monetary improvements in pay disappear in real terms as others demand and receive similar improvements so that costs and prices are forced up, usually in rough proportion to the rise in wage-costs.

Just as one kind of inflation—demand inflation—reflects a failure to expand production in line with the additional claims on it, and a disturbance in the balance between supply and demand, so the other kind of inflation—cost inflation—reflects a failure to change the distribution of income in favour of those laying claim to higher pay. In both cases the essential inflation is in claims in relation to the possibility of satisfying them. Either the economy labours and overheats under undue pressure or inflation sorts out the excessive claims that are entered when there is no general agreement on how the national income should be distributed.

Wages are not the only element in cost and, even if they were, prices might rise faster than costs because profit margins were increasing. Whatever the historical experience on this point governments rarely try to control wages without controlling prices simultaneously, presumably because they want to reassure wage-earners that their acceptance of less advantageous wage bargains will not be offset by a corresponding widening of profit margins. It may be a valid political judgement that price control has to accompany wage control; but there is very little reason nowadays to regard a widening of profit margins or profiteering as an important cause rather than a common symptom of inflation.

Other sources of cost inflation have also to be considered. Recent events have brought home the powerful inflationary influence that can be exerted by an exogenous rise in the price of foodstuffs and materials. This rise can be on a scale well beyond any recent increase from year to year in the level of wages; and when it comes through into the level of consumer prices is bound to provoke claims for higher wages and so inflate prices still further. In the distant past this kind of influence on prices was episodic and associated with harvest failure. But with the growth of an international economy in which world-wide crop failures are unlikely to occur and local shortages can be made good by importation, cost inflation from the side of foodstuffs and materials has a different origin and can rarely be explained in terms of the circumstances of a single country. Instead it directs our attention to what is going on in the rest of the world and the wider problem of the transmission of inflation from country to country.

Inflation—whether demand inflation or cost inflation—can be due either to purely domestic influences or to external influences, or to a mixture of the two. Until recently the emphasis put on domestic as opposed to international influences depended very much on the size and openness of a country's economy on the one hand and the state of its balance of payments on the other. A small country, particularly one linked closely with its neighbours, was very much exposed to the prevailing economic climate in the major economies dominating the world economy. It was bound, therefore, to be more alive to the danger of importing inflation from them when they were undergoing over-rapid expansion. On the other hand, deficit countries, especially if they ranked among the major economies, were apt to beat their breasts and regard inflation as something of their own making. In the United Kingdom, for example, explanations of inflation tend to be cast year after year in terms of some local failing, to the almost complete exclusion of what is going on in other countries. In spite of the preoccupation of British economic policy with international trade and payments ever since World War Two, discussions of inflation by British economists and economic journalists usually run in terms more appropriate to a closed economy. In the Netherlands, Germany and other continental countries where prices have risen nearly as steeply, the emphasis is very different and frequently implies that inflation is an imported good (or evil) manufactured in the United States. The fact that prices rose less rapidly there than in Western Europe through the sixties is not thought to be inconsistent with this view.

Now it is quite true that every country cannot explain away its own inflation by pointing at the rest of the world: what is one country's import must be some other country's export. In that sense a final explanation has to be applicable to a closed economy since the world as a whole *is* a closed economy. It is also true that some countries form a much larger component of the world economy than others and they may call the tune. Domestic influences in those major countries—the half dozen or so largest members of the OECD—then become the focus of attention. These influences may operate directly to produce inflation domestically and thereafter be transmitted abroad or they may exert pressure on foreign economies that are already under strain and set off an inflation of prices there. While we ought to look at the major economies first we cannot necessarily confine our attention to them. Even if we could do so in normal circumstances, there are bound to be abnormal circumstances, of which the recent jacking up of oil prices provides a striking example, and we may then have to look first at the non-industrial countries if we want to unravel the inflationary process.

IV

We have to explain not only why the post-war world has experienced continuous inflation, but why there has been such an acceleration of the process over the past few years. Let us separate the two questions chronologically in terms of the years before and after 1967 when the pound was devalued.

If we look back to the middle of the last century we can see that the course of prices has been upwards except in two periods, one between 1873 and 1896 and one between 1920 and 1933. The first of these periods was one in which there was a rapid reduction in the delivered cost of imported primary produce because of improvements in transport and the opening up of cheaper sources of supply. Money wages in the industrial countries continued to rise but not at the rate that would have been required to hold the cost of living steady. There was some slack in the labour market but a gradual rise in real wages. In most years, employers were neither in such acute competition for labour that they offered higher wages, nor under such pressure from wage earners that they had to concede to them. The years between the two world wars, for rather different reasons, did not give rise to inflationary wage settlements. In Britain, for example, unemployment, as then measured, hardly ever fell below 10 per cent in the twenties and after 1929 rose to much larger proportions.

From 1933 onwards, however, in spite of heavy unemployment, money wages increased and the trend in the price of foodstuffs and materials was reversed. The result was a gradual rise in prices throughout a period of continuing industrial depression. In the United Kingdom weekly wage-rates between June 1933 and June 1939 rose by 11 per cent compared with a fall of over 6 per cent during the six preceding years. In view of some of the arguments now current about the responsiveness of wage inflation to conditions in the labour market it is as well to remember that unemployment during those years of rising wages and prices was consistently in excess of 10 per cent.

Post-war experience has not, therefore, been so completely different from pre-war as is sometimes implied. But there has been a more continuous rise in prices then any experienced over the preceding century. There can be little doubt as to the reason for this continuity. It lies in the conditions of almost continuous boom, *alias* full employment, in all the major industrial countries ever since 1945. In the United Kingdom, for example, there has been no year since the war in which the national product failed to increase. If the demand for labour is sustained in this way it is hardly surprising if wages keep going up and if they do it is still less surprising that people should expect the process to go on more or less without interruption—freezes in wages and prices apart. Continuous pressure, reinforced by the expectation of continuous pressure, creates a climate of opinion in which wage increases do not greatly check the demand for labour but become the basis for a fresh rise in prices. Governments are known to be committed to full employment so that employers as a group have no reason to fear that higher wages will destroy their markets although some employers may fear that the concessions asked of them will be excessive in relation to wage changes either in other industries or in competing industries abroad.

This is no more than to say, what Beveridge said long ago, that full employment transforms the bargaining situation and puts power to dictate the movement of wages in the hands of the workers and their representatives. Of course to some extent this is an illusion because increases in money wages are not transformed into real wages and are cancelled out once employers adjust their prices. The rate of increase in real wages remains obstinately close to the upward trend in output per head and is a function of the success of the Government in sustaining full employment far more than of the success of the workers in exploiting their additional bargaining power.

v

If next we look at the experience of the past six years or so there is no need for me to elaborate on the acceleration that has taken place in the fall in the value of money. An average increase in consumer prices of 3–4 per cent in most industrial countries has now increased to 10–15 per cent or more. It is not possible to blame this acceleration on the Arabs since it was already observable well before October 1973. It can be ascribed to the sharp increase in international liquidity, i.e. there is a monetary explanation. It can be put down to heavier pressure on world capacity, i.e. to demand factors. Or it can be explained in terms of a more intense struggle to resolve distributional claims. It is possible to find evidence for all of these explanations.

There is no doubt, for example, about the very large increase in the level of world reserves of gold and foreign exchange since 1967. Even without revaluing gold from its official price of $35–40 to its present market price of over $160, world liquidity increased in the four years between the end of 1969 and the end of 1973 by over 140 per cent. This brought with it a large expansion in domestic liquidity in the countries gaining reserves since they were rarely able (and did not always try very hard) to offset the immediate impact on the monetary system. It also shifted the balance between surplus and deficit countries since few countries could be in deficit in a world creating international money at such a fantastic rate. Hence, on the one hand inflationary influences were strengthened through domestic credit creation and the constraints that external deficits would have introduced were simultaneously relaxed. Without suggesting that these monetary factors were of overriding importance they undoubtedly operated strongly in an expansionist (and in the circumstances) inflationary direction.

There are reasons for supposing that demand pressures would have increased even in the absence of greater world liquidity. These pressures have been common with few exceptions to all industrial countries as the expansion in each country synchronised with and supported expansion in its neighbours. The local pressures generated were transmitted abroad and were in turn reinforced by the total international situation. This situation was dominated by the instability of the dollar and the acceleration of inflation in the United States, by far the largest single component of the Western world. Until the Vietnam war, the dollar had provided a stable international currency and prices in the US market had operated as a brake on the movement of commodity prices elsewhere. The United States economy was in this way a convenient point of reference to which other economies could adjust. But from the late sixties and, still more, after the abandonment of a fixed parity in August 1971, this source of international stability was lost.

Almost simultaneously with the unhitching of the dollar from gold there began an unusually sustained and widespread expansion in activity that coincided in the main industrial countries to a greater extent than in earlier post-war booms. The upswing was intensified by speculation in the commodity markets—speculation that was itself a product of inflation and fear of inflation. Thus quite apart from the effect of specific shortages, monopolistic influences and wage-push, the stage was set for an unusually large rise in prices and for a continuation of the rise once in progress.

The rise in commodity prices that set in towards the end of 1972 is without precedent in peace time if we set aside the scramble for raw materials in 1950–51 during the Korean war. In less than eighteen months the export price of primary produce increased by something like 80 per cent and this was translated into an almost equally sharp rise in delivered costs in the importing countries. It is possible to interpret this upswing, as I have suggested, as the outcome of a world boom reinforced by speculation and to support this view by showing that the terms of trade between primary produce and manufactured goods have merely returned to where they were in the 1950s. But one cannot help suspecting that, underneath the speculative pressure, longer-term forces have been at work bringing into relief the limited sources of some of the major primary products. The similar shift in the balance between demand and supply was most vividly apparent in the changes at work in the United States which made her either less self-sufficient (e.g. in petroleum) or a less abundant reservoir of exports (e.g. of grain). Cyclical expansion in other words, encountered an unusually inelastic supply.

It may well be that this inelasticity has been aggravated by abnormal circumstances: by deliberate restriction of output imposed under conditions of over-supply; by concern for environmental damage and a consequent delay in the opening up of new sources of supply; by the cartelisation of the Arab oil producers. Making all allowances for exceptional factors, the events of 1972–3 may still be symptomatic of a deeper change in the market for primary products. On the analogy of the similar change that took place in the middle nineties of the last century the transition is one calculated to intensify inflationary trends.

The forces at work in the monetary system and in commodity markets were reinforced by inflationary forces in the labour market. Full employment, economic growth, and rising expectations combined to generate an atmosphere of militancy all over the world. Wage demands were urged with greater force as the pre-war generation of workers died out and as affluence enlarged expectations. The greater bargaining power and greater militancy of wage earners made it inevitable that they would resist any sudden set-back in their real income such as higher commodity prices involved and would seek to transfer the burden of dearer imports to other shoulders by scaling up their wage demands. In entering these claims the workers were bound also to try to protect themselves against unpredictable further changes in the value of money. This usually meant claiming wages high enough to match their worst fears.

Although the rise in commodity prices brought into play a sharper struggle over distribution of income, it is doubtful whether the tug-of-war in the labour market would of itself have produced the kind of acceleration experienced in the past two years. That is, it seems reasonable to regard our present difficulties as in large measure a hangover from the spurt in commodity prices and the monetary and demand pressures that generated it. It would be quite consistent wth this view of things to insist that the long-term outlook remains extremely serious and that alike in the commodity markets and in the labour market the prospect is one of an accelerating rise in costs.

VI

Economists used to be attacked, with some reason, for having no satisfactory theory with which to explain *unemployment* and devise remedies for it. They are now open to attack, with less reason, for having too many theories of *inflation* and no satisfactory remedy for it. To my mind they would be wise to admit at least the second half of the charge. They ought to give up the pretence that inflation is a purely economic disorder to be explained and treated exclusively in economic terms. It is no more a purely economic phenomenon than economic growth, the roots of which also lie outside traditional economics. The fact that we measure inflation and growth in terms of economic variables and that both have conspicuous economic consequences should not mislead us into looking for their cause and cure within the same narrow limits.

Inflation has its origin in social and political quite as much as in economic factors. It grows out of the aspirations and expectations of the mass of the population. These find political expression in the assertion of rights and are not confined to the lodging of claims. A world in which incomes are regarded as fixed by custom and the forces of the market is giving way to one in which they are seen to be increasingly dependent on the actions of government. Nearly everybody thinks themselves entitled to more income than they get; and although collectively they cannot get more than they produce, they can demand more and take action in support of their demands. The inflation which this produces is the economic component of an unsuccessfully managed (perhaps unmanageable) society. In the inter-war years the political reality was concealed by heavy unemployment which destroyed any inflationary expectations. But in the post-war world, unemployment is itself part of the package that governments are expected to deliver and can have only a limited restraining effect on aspirations to higher incomes.

What is at issue is the distribution of income in a democratic society and it is no longer possible to pretend that this is settled by economic forces alone. It is only too obvious that the State can determine, to a far greater extent than was once thought possible, how the national cake shall be divided. With its enormous powers to tax and spend the State can channel income this way and that, to the disadvantage of one group and the advantage of another, without necessarily involving itself very deeply in the process by which individuals strike the bargains that determine their gross incomes. It is inevitable that this display of its powers should strike the imagination of individual bargainers and raise questions in their minds over the outcome of that bargaining. It becomes increasingly difficult to hold to a rigorous separation of the two processes by which net incomes are determined; the fixing of gross incomes through the haggling of the market and the subsequent cutting down or enlargement of these incomes through the operations of government.

On the one hand, therefore, we have a steady expansion in public expenditure as the implications of the welfare state unfold and rising expectations are met by rising public provision; while on the other hand we have a steady (or accelerating) inflation of money incomes as rising expectations are translated into higher and higher wage-claims. The first kind of expansion is real because the State has the power to obtain command over the necessary resources by taxation or social service contributions; the second kind of expansion is largely illusory because settlements for higher wages are undone by later settlements and the consequent rise in prices. So long as other forms of income are not squeezed, inflation sees to it that real wages will not rise faster than productivity, and for bringing about a squeeze the budget is far more powerful than collective bargaining. Nevertheless once the merry-go-round of inflation starts, the fragmentation of collective bargaining into a succession of negotiations means that it will carry on under its own momentum; and the gap between the improvements expected and the improvements within reach may generate increasing frustration and a steady increase in the size of the increments demanded.

It is natural to suggest that in these circumstances an effort should be made to establish a more orderly process for distributing the national income. Sometimes, as in Sweden, the effort may be limited to the framing of a comprehensive bargain between the organisations of employers and employed, leaving the details to be settled in the light of local circumstances. In Britain a more ambitious type of bargain is now in vogue in the form of a social compact between the government and the TUC. Perhaps something enduring will emerge from this experiment. But there can obviously be no guarantee that it makes it easier to contain inflationary aspirations by throwing in the powers of the State to gratify them. Market forces have their own logic and it is not the same as the logic of Parliamentary debate.

VII

So what are we to do about it? First of all, we may be tempted to offer the advice of Hilaire Belloc's doctors who:

> . . . murmured as they took their fees
> There is no cure for this disease.

If so, we are in for a bad time and the prophets of dictatorship, whether of the left or of the right, can count on a large and growing following.

Without going quite so far, we may accept the inevitability of an unusually severe and prolonged attack and yet hope to see it followed in a year or two by a spell of what might be called convalescence. It is highly unlikely that international commodity prices will continue to mount at anything like so rapid a rate as over the past year or so and they may well fall from their present level. Perhaps, therefore, we ought to be patient and treat the present inflation as a fever that will gradually abate if we take proper precautions. There have been times in the past, like the early fifties, when inflation took on alarming proportions largely because of a speculative commodity boom, and yet within a few years the pace of inflation had fallen back to a relatively slow and acceptable rate. Might not the same happen again? Would it not be wise to recognise that, whatever the long run trend, there are some exceptional and unsustainable elements in the present inflation and prepare ourselves for at least a temporary subsidence in the wake of a retreat from the boom conditions of 1973?

Secondly, we should be on our guard against magic and automatic

82   *Inflation, Growth and International Finance*

devices that claim to put an end to inflation at a stroke. The sirens among us will continue to sing of what might be done by a return to the gold standard, tighter money, nationally and internationally, fixed annual increments in the money supply, balanced budgets, freer markets, and the host of more exotic, nostalgic, or mystical remedies that pop up in my postbag. But governments that want to be re-elected will hesitate to entrust their future to a formula that in one form or another is bound to spell restriction. They have listened in the past to expansionary ditties like the call for faster growth at a predetermined rate that drew them irresistibly on to inflationary rocks. They may steer for Scylla again: but why should they choose Charybdis instead?

Yet I would not dispute the inflationary bias of the international economic system so long as countries are free to put full employment ahead of other objectives and obligations and have found no way of combining full employment and price stability. Sooner or later governments will have to resume some of the power over the value of their currency which they have forfeited by underwriting full employment unconditionally. Where they are in chronic deficit, as many now are, they may think it prudent to reduce their vulnerability by reducing the pressure on their capacity for the time being. They may also wish to re-examine the pressure that they can maintain in the longer run without aggravating inflation. This is not, as I have explained, a matter of a fixed curve from which one can read off the behaviour of wages and prices once one knows the level of unemployment. It is a question rather of a shifting danger-zone within which wage bargaining begins to reflect strongly the influence of demand factors. There are grounds for arguing that, whatever was possible ten or twenty years ago, an attempt to combine 2 per cent unemployment and 2 per cent inflation is not possible now; and that it would be more in keeping with a true appreciation of the long-term dangers to accept for a time the risk of somewhat higher levels of unemployment.

Thirdly, it would be easier to gain acceptance of this if a greater effort were made to re-train and re-employ those falling out of employment. This would increase the mobility of labour and make it possible to sustain a higher pressure without producing the shortages and bottlenecks that become transformed into higher wages and prices. What is now thought of as man-power policy is an indispensable element in a comprehensive attempt to master inflation.

Fourthly, collective bargaining in its present form is inconsistent with price stability and the only question worth discussing is how we can modify collective bargaining without forfeiting its advantages. The various attempts to devise a satisfactory incomes policy have not been particularly successful and there are no simple and acceptable answers. But in my view we should not give up trying.

Finally, a small country with an open economy cannot help being at the mercy of inflationary impulses transmitted from abroad. However it tries to screen itself from these impulses by monetary policy, flexible exchange rates, social compacts, and other still more sophisticated devices, it cannot escape the consequences of others' failings. This is so even if it manages its own affairs in an ideal non-inflationary way. All it can do is to set a good example and pray that others will do so too.

Chapter 5

Incomes Policy

Retrospect and Prospect[1]

'When the poor feel as poor as the rich do, there will be a bloody revolution.' Rebecca West, *The Thinking Reed*

'If you want to destroy Capitalism, debauch the currency.'
Attributed to Lenin by Keynes

Few things in economic policy excite stronger and more divergent responses than the efforts of governments to control directly the movement of prices and incomes. There are those who favour an incomes policy almost without regard to what it is or how it works, as if it were a kind of ju-ju that need only be produced to scare away inflation. There are others who think it economic nonsense, misguided and mischievous. It has been attacked by some as unnecessary, by others as unworkable or ineffective, and by others again as calculated to sow discord or to aggravate rather than moderate inflation.

These differences of opinion are as pronounced among professional economists as among laymen of all persuasions. One can point to Lord Balogh, Lord Roberthall and Sir Roy Harrod among the enthusiasts and to Gunnar Myrdal and Milton Friedman among the sceptics. There are other curious alliances: the virtues of free collective bargaining are almost the only thing on which Enoch Powell and the TUC see eye to eye. There are also dramatic conversions: not only changes of view by individual economists like Professor Paish but the extraordinary *volte-face* that led a Conservative government dedicated to non-intervention to take wider powers in 1972–3 to control prices and incomes than any government enjoyed in this country for at least twenty-five years.

THE RECORD OF THE 1960s

The historical record is not encouraging. Throughout the various phases of incomes policy there has been a wide divergence between

[1]Originally published in the *Three Banks Review* (December 1973).

the actual movement of prices and earnings and the movement laid down as desirable by the Government. Except for the short freezes by which the policy has been punctuated, it is difficult to point to any inflection in the upward curve that shows the unmistakable influence of the policy itself. Even the concentration of Ministerial time and energy under the Labour Government of 1964–70 failed almost completely to make reality accord with policy. In spite of no less than six White Papers between 1965 and 1970, each enunciating a new norm for the movement of incomes or new criteria for exceptional treatment, the rise in money incomes and prices was faster over those five years than over the preceding five years. As Hugh Clegg has pointed out

'during 1965 and the first half of 1966, when the norm was 3% to 3½%, weekly earnings were rising at about 8% a year. During 1967, with a zero norm, or no norm, and all increases requiring exceptional justification, the increase was about 6%. In 1968 and 1969, with a ceiling of 3½%, the rate of growth returned to the 1965 level. Judged by these figures the whole policy was a colossal failure.'[1]

The National Board for Prices and Incomes, set up in 1965, never claimed more for its efforts than that inflation had been slowed down by perhaps 1 per cent per annum. Many would regard this judgement as too optimistic. They would claim that the concentration of the Labour Government on incomes policy and its consequent deferment of deflationary measures by nearly two years after it took office in 1964, accelerated the rise in wages and prices, making the devaluation of 1967 more rather than less necessary. Whatever one makes of these claims and counter-claims, they do nothing to upset the common view that incomes policy, viewed as an anti-inflationary device, came nowhere near measuring up to the hopes and expectations that were placed in it.

One reason for this is that the policy was at once too vague and too ambitious. It was too vague because the mechanism by which it was to operate was left largely in obscurity. It was too ambitious because the various guiding lights, norms and ceilings that were announced were related almost exclusively to what was necessary in order to stabilise prices and not at all to the rate at which prices had in fact been increasing.

No attempt was made in the 1960s to reassure those who feared that their willingness to accept a stringent limit on increases in their pay might not be matched by an equal willingness on the part of

[1] Hugh Clegg, *How to Run an Incomes Policy*, p. 13.

others, so that prices might continue to rise and offset, or more than offset, a rise in pay within the limits of the norm. On the contrary, it was part of the policy not to encourage indexation of wages and other incomes; and the norm was not specified or elaborated in such a way as to cover only partial success of the policy.

Throughout most of the post-war period the policy has been a voluntary one, that may not unfairly be summarised as prayers and incantations with the addition now and then of a little arsenic in the form of a wage freeze or pay pause. From the days of Stafford Cripps onwards there was a disposition to enunciate a few general principles, such as that wages should rise no faster than productivity, and to leave it to collective bargaining to interpret the principles. The White Paper of February 1948, for example, took the line that there was no justification for any general increase in individual money incomes but accepted the need for wage increases in industries that were ' undermanned'. It did not explain to whom justification should be offered nor what penalties would attend infringement of the principle. Instead, it relied on sweet reason and goodwill. Similarly, both the Conservative and the Labour Governments in the early 1960s thought of incomes policy primarily as an exercise in public education. No indication of any powers to implement the policy is written into the famous *Statement of Intent* which George Brown and both the CBI and the TUC signed in December 1964. Even when the Prices and Incomes Board came into existence in 1965 it had no power to determine its own references and no authority like that enjoyed by the Pay Board or the Price Commission in 1973 to issue definitive rulings based on a statutory code.

WAGE FREEZES

Whether the policy has been voluntary or statutory, the one thing that does seem to work while it lasts is a wage freeze. There are now three examples of this: the freeze that overlapped the devaluation of 1949, when the TUC undertook to hold wages even if prices rose by up to 5 per cent; the freeze that accompanied the deflationary measures taken in July 1966; and the freeze introduced in 1972 as a prelude to the re-introduction of an incomes policy. In all three cases the background of the freeze was a crisis of some kind that helped to secure general acceptance. The pay pause introduced by Mr Selwyn Lloyd in 1961 was unsuccessful partly because there was no similar sense of crisis and partly because of the emphasis which was put on wage restraint in the public sector without regard to the reception given to the Government's call for a pay pause in the private sector.

Experience suggests that the effectiveness and acceptability of a standstill in incomes tend to decline rather rapidly. It is true that the freeze may extend, under very favourable circumstances such as those of 1948–50, up to a year or so; but as a rule six months appears to be the limit. People are willing to postpone their claims for a limited period when everyone seems to be treated alike. But as anomalies accumulate, exceptions have to be made and the appearance of equity is difficult to preserve. Wage drift in one form or another creates tension between those who benefit from it and those who do not and this tension is often most acute in some of the higher-paid industries. If import prices go on rising, this affects foodstuffs and other items of special importance to the lower-paid workers and creates resentment there too. In addition, the political will and determination behind the freeze begin to wilt. Proposals for moderation cannot be presented in the same light and do not arouse the same enthusiasm as a general stop affecting everyone alike. After a time, therefore, there is usually a reaction against any form of restraint and what passes as incomes policy, as distinct from a freeze, is ushered in just as opinion is veering round in the opposite direction.

The check to the expansion in money incomes in a freeze is visible enough. But inflation goes on in other ways. There are ladders across the ice provided by systems of payment by results, local agreements that escape challenge and long-term wage agreements that have not been suspended. These confer advantages on some groups of workers who for the time being outdistance the others. When the freeze is over the distance between the two can be closed by larger claims from those who have been left behind and the drag on the upward movement of earnings then turns out to bear little relation to the size of the initial check.

PHASES I AND II

Nothing happened in 1973 to upset this conclusion. Emergency action to introduce a freeze was successful in the sense that it was widely accepted as a means of breaking the rhythm of inflationary expectations and it did, for the time being, check the rise in wages and prices. Even in Phase II there was no major challenge to the policy (unless one counts the demonstrations organised by the trade unions for— of all days—May 1). But the success was at best partial. Consumer prices rose 10 per cent in twelve months and wage rates 15 per cent.

These rates are comparable with the highest in any post-war year (or for that matter any year in World War Two): hardly a triumph for a policy intended to control inflation.

It is easy to explain away this outcome by pointing to the course of international prices: the rise in import prices by over 30 per cent in a year, the doubling of commodity prices, the swing in the terms of trade of no less than 15 per cent against the United Kingdom. It was a highly exceptional year and no incomes policy could have avoided severe inflation under the circumstances. But it would be wrong to dismiss experience in 1973 quite so swiftly. For it brings out very strikingly how limited the scope for incomes policy as an anti-inflationary device may be. Apart altogether from the problems of making the policy fair and effective there is the need to combine it with policies aimed at regulating the pressure of demand and insulating the economy as far as possible from fluctuations abroad.

This would be difficult enough in any circumstances. But if both demand management and exchange rate policy are dominated by the British obsession with growth there is little that incomes policy can do. The determination to keep on expanding demand after the pressure has reached danger point has immediate and obvious effects on prices, wages and the balance of payments long before they can be checked by any theoretical gains in productivity—and, particularly with a static labour force that dampens any benefits to the economy from increasing returns, these gains (properly measured) are likely to remain theoretical. The deficit in the balance of payments—and so prolonging the boom with other people's money—puts it in turn beyond the power of the Government to ward off any simultaneous rise in prices abroad by appreciating the currency. Not that this has much practical importance. The Government, egged on by the TUC and the CBI, is usually all too anxious to let the rate slide anyhow in pursuit of that other will-o'-the-wisp, export-led growth. Since the slow rate of growth in Britain has very little to do either with demand management or with floating exchange rates it is hardly surprising if the upshot is accelerating inflation, punctuated by exchange crises, without any visible dividend in faster growth and with frequent recourse to emergency action to hold down costs by means of incomes policy.

It would take us too far afield to develop these points, or to apply them to the highly dangerous situation that the prevailing economic mythology has created. But if incomes policy is to be put in perspective it is important to get away from the idea that wage restraint by itself will curb inflation. It is no use thinking that the same remedy can be applied to a boom like 1964–5, a wage explosion like 1969–70 and an international scramble for commodities like 1950–1 or 1972–4. In different types of situation the scope for incomes policy and the appropriate type of incomes policy are bound to vary. In almost *any* situation the inflationary process is fed from many different quarters—employers bidding for more labour, workers pushing for higher wages, foreign suppliers raising commodity prices, governments increasing taxes—and each party may feel the innocent victim of what the others are doing. International *and* domestic factors, wage-pull *and* wage-push, are normally at work simultaneously, and controls at one point may only add to the pressure at another.

There is, for example, no fixed point in the tightening of the labour market at which demand inflation takes off and supersedes any previous wage-push and no fixed point in the process of slackening at which demand pressures disappear completely, exposing the uncomplicated workings of trade union militancy. There is nearly always pressure on capacity somewhere in the system to give leverage to wages and nearly always some scope for tougher bargaining throughout the system. So while at some times the running may be made *predominantly* by demand and prices and at other times *predominantly* by wages and costs, there is a rather confusing mixture of the two, particularly in the neighbourhood of full employment.

Any attempt to take hold of the situation by controlling prices only is liable to prove unworkable because the element of wage-push will continue to operate and cut unequally into the profit margins to which the productive system responds; any attempt to take hold by controlling wages only is liable to create labour shortages in essential services and delay in adaptation of the pattern of output to market requirements. In any event both employers and workers will resist control as endangering their livelihood. They are likely to take diametrically opposite views of the complex interplay of prices and wages and disclaim responsibility for feeding the inflationary spiral.

The influence of international factors is also constantly at work, in ways that have been far too little studied, transmitting inflation from one country to another. Changes in foreign demand, in commodity prices, in international capital flows, or in exchange rates exert pressure on the domestic price structure and open up new opportunities or justifications for higher wage bargains that may set a new norm for wage-settlements. In some of the smaller countries such as Sweden, the pace of inflation is largely dictated by the behaviour of the international sector; and unless the labour unions are to acquiesce in a substantial shift to profits they have little option but to press for large additions to money wages when the international sector is booming. They can defend such action under those circumstances as non-inflationary, i.e. as profiting from, rather than causing, higher prices. But the difficulty is that higher wages justified in one sector by exceptional profits become generalised throughout the economy on grounds of fairness between one group of workers and another.

THE TWO-WAY STRETCH IN WAGE CLAIMS

This two-way stretch is in some ways the nub of the whole problem. The labour market is dominated on the one hand by relativities that resist change and are generated as much by a strong sense of equity as by the forces of the market: and on the other hand by the efforts of workers to share in the business success of the firm or industry in which they are engaged—but only in a direction that carries their rates of pay upwards, never downwards. It needs only limited success in these efforts, reflected in one or two important wage settlements, for the rest of the labour force to take its cue and exert itself to restore the previous relativities. Once employers have reacted in turn by adjusting their prices to what is a fairly uniform increase in labour costs, the only significant change accomplished is a fall in the value of money.

It might seem that such a situation could be readily dealt with, provided the trade unions would co-operate in holding wages in different occupations and industries in some agreed relationship with one another, leaving the balance between wages, profits and other incomes to be settled through taxation. But the matter is not quite so simple. The powers of trade unions over wages are limited. In the case of prices there is general recognition of the extreme decentralisation of the process by which they are fixed and the consequent difficulty of government control. It is this that accounts for the widespread conviction that price control is essentially an elaborate charade unless confined to the larger firms, backed by a common willingness or eagerness to comply, and preferably combined with other controls such as were used in wartime over variety of product, supply of materials, and so on. What is not so well understood is that a great deal of the same argumentation applies to wages. This is because the trade unions are thought to exercise a control over the supply and price of labour that has no counterpart in the market for the goods produced. But the powers of trade unions over their members are just as limited as the powers of employers' associations over theirs; and what is more to the point, trade unions play very little part in some of the most inflationary settlements in British industry and have even less influence over them.

PLANT BARGAINING

The average worker's pay packet in Britain is fixed as to about half by wage agreements at national level between trade unions and employers' associations. Most of the other half is settled within the plant. Much the same ratio applies to the proportion of the increase in the wage bill from year to year that is regulated by national agreements. Again, as was shown by the National Board for Prices and Incomes in its Report on *Payment by Results* in 1968, half the increase in wages (leaving overtime payments out of income) normally results from negotiations at plant level. For the middle sixties this element in wage increases was as large as the underlying rate of improvement in national productivity (the source of true economic growth). In other words, these supplementary payments alone absorbed as much additional purchasing power as would have been consistent with stable prices at the current rate of growth in economic potential.

The bargaining that controls the size of these payments may go on between the foreman or ratefixer and the individual worker (over piece prices), between supervisors and groups of workers, or between the management and the shop stewards. Trade union officials are rarely directly concerned and may never so much as set foot in the plant. Over 40 per cent of workers in manufacturing in Britain are on payment by results and their pay is only loosely related to the terms of national agreements. This is not to say that they do not benefit like other workers from these agreements. But the degree of managerial control over what they earn per week is often minimal and is commonly governed by a highly uncertain process calculated to generate anomalies and inflame feelings of unfairness. Some economists would argue that these payments systems and the drift that goes with them are quite enough to account for most of the inflation that went on in the fifties and sixties and that if incomes policy was ineffective over that period this may have been because it never came to grips with inflation at the plant level.

WAGE DRIFT

In the fixing of piece rates there is ample scope for continuous pressure by individual workers or groups of workers, particularly where changes are taking place in working arrangements through innovations in products, materials, machines, or methods. The wage drift in which this results is not a function of additional effort on the part of the wage-earner nor does it fluctuate very closely with the level of unemployment in the neighbourhood. It is the outcome of repeated re-negotiation of rates in a weak bargaining situation traceable in the last resort to full or near-full employment. The drift is intensified when activity on the shop floor is expanding and must to some extent reflect the changing pressure of demand. But, as with nationally agreed rates of wages, changes in demand are only one of the factors at work and drift does not cease when output is steady any more than wages rates cease to rise under these conditions.

The fact of wage drift, divorced from the activities of organised labour, means that pressure is exerted throughout the wage structure independently of any bargaining between trade unions and employers. Tension is created within the industries making use of payments by results, between piece-workers who profit from drift and time-workers who do not. The tension extends to workers in other industries who can make comparison with piece-work earnings. Once relativities are disturbed, there are strong forces working to restore them. In all countries the wage structure shows a remarkable rigidity over time. Hence, it can be argued that the whole inflationary merry-go-round is set in motion by wage drift in industries like the motor-car industry that make use of payment by results and experience rapid technical change: that inflation, like so many other things, is 'made in Coventry'.

Whatever the bargaining mechanism—whether on the shop floor or in negotiations with powerful unions—the fundamental change that has occurred is in the expectation of full employment and consequent freedom to press for a better wage bargain. If piece rates were replaced by time rates, inflation would not cease. Nor would it cease if trade unions were weaker. It has been obvious ever since the war that full employment was likely to lead to inflation and that this need not be a matter of demand pressure but could equally well be due to the realisation by groups of workers of their power to push up money wages so long as governments acted to sustain employment.

Many people continue to assume that wage bargaining is entirely between trade unions and employers. But this is nonsense. On the one hand, it neglects what is happening on the shop floor; on the other hand, it ignores the meetings at Chequers and No. 10 Downing Street.

MACRO-ECONOMIC BARGAINING

Incomes policy has introduced the Government into the bargaining situation because it has an interest in checking inflation. But there has been in Britain a reciprocal effect since the unions feel entitled to bargain about incomes policy. It is easy to see that if something called incomes policy is invoked as an anti-inflationary weapon, it is impossible to use it for long without reference to broad issues of distributional justice. Equally, it is difficult to divorce any discussion of the growth of money incomes from policies affecting the growth of real incomes; and if this is thought to depend on the Government's management of the economy then this, too, automatically becomes involved in incomes policy. Once debate starts on the equity or appropriateness of efforts to control money incomes, it can range over a succession of issues of social and economic policy without much hope of finality and leave the parties to the debate arguing over fundamentally different views about the form of society instead of concentrating on the specific evil of inflation.

Hence, when employers and unions are called to No. 10 Downing Street there tends to be a very wide agenda. The unions have sought to introduce questions of demand management, pensions, control of profits and dividends, repeal of the Industrial Relations Act, and so on.

The parties to a discussion of this kind may fool the public but they do not fool themselves. There is no general acceptance of the need for a continuing machinery to control prices and incomes. Employers are not reconciled to indefinite price control; the unions still insist on the need to resume free collective bargaining; the Government is in no hurry to put its powers of economic management in commission. Each party is playing for position and reluctant to force a showdown; as has happened in the past, however, external pressures may drive one party or the other to take independent action and put an end to any chance of agreement.

The fact is that events are not within the control of the parties to the negotiations to the degree necessary for their success. The CBI does not fix prices and its influence, even on the larger employers, is limited; the TUC does not fix wages and its influence on wage claims is very limited indeed; the Government does not have the kind of influence on economic growth or the power to predict the response of the economy to its own policies that is required in order to underwrite the promises demanded of it. As the events of 1973–4 have shown—for example, the swing in the current account of £5,000m.— external events may eat up the Government's room for manoeuvre and destroy the credibility of its policies. Both employers and unions may be held back by fears of their constituents' reactions from offering the active (or even tacit) co-operation that the policy requires. The Boards administering the Code may be hamstrung by forces outside their control and obliged to ratify increases in prices and wages which make a mockery of their presumed functions.

STATUTORY POWERS AND SANCTIONS

The Government knows that it cannot make use of outright compulsion except for very limited purposes and periods. It may assume statutory powers but the sanctions on which it can draw are not very effective. They can be applied more readily to prices than to pay. A large firm may feel obliged to comply with rulings as to prices and would rarely seek to challenge the Government openly; it cannot be compelled to produce at a loss but it may even be willing to go that far for a limited time rather than sacrifice goodwill. On the other hand, when trade unions or any group of employees go on strike, they can defy the Government without much added inconvenience and may even welcome the confrontation with authority (particularly under a Conservative Government) or the prospect of martyrdom. Workers cannot be forced to work and their leaders cannot in practice be imprisoned even when they have broken the law. There is no help in legal injunctions or sets of legal penalties unless the law is sustained by public opinion; and in Britain the mass of wage-earners are not inclined to endorse the use of legal penalties against strikes or infringement of industrial agreements. The working man is inclined to regard lawyers with suspicion and react against the intrusion of the law into industrial relations.

The essence of the British situation is that voluntary policies have not worked; that freezes of one kind or another appear at the time to be effective but in retrospect are less successful than they seemed; and that statutory powers can in the end be employed only with the acquiescence of the unions. They have been willing to accept a freeze because it is a temporary affair and suspends collective bargaining without professing to supersede it. What they are not prepared to do is to surrender on a continuing footing their right to engage in free collective bargaining on behalf of their members. Economists may regard this as a prescription for 'a South American future' and throw doubt on any gains in real wages that such freedom brings. Businessmen may rage against 'a tedious process of disorderly legalised extortion'. But the unions are not as yet prepared to envisage or accept long-term institutional arrangements that limit their powers. They are certainly unwilling to acquiesce in any policy conceived exclusively in terms of wage restraint.

THE FUTURE OF INCOMES POLICY

What then is to be done? Any worthwhile policy must have long-run aims and is unlikely to be of much help for immediate purposes.

First of all, there should be no turning back from the efforts to find a satisfactory framework for incomes policy. In Britain (whatever may be possible in Sweden) these efforts are bound to involve the Government directly as well as indirectly, and must probably originate with the Government. Since it is by far the largest paymaster in the country it cannot divest itself of the responsibilities of an employer and wash its hands of wages and prices: the sheer size of the public sector rules this out. But it has other and wider responsibilities, not least as the guarantor of full employment and a powerful prop of the bargaining power of labour. It cannot sit idly by if this bargaining power is used to determine the pace of inflation; and it cannot be expected to adapt everything else in the economy to the rise in money incomes, especially if the rise is serving no purpose except to debase the currency.

Secondly, the Government will be successful in its efforts the more it can command the support of public opinion. It must, therefore, set out to arouse and mobilise opinion behind an intelligible policy that can be shown to be necessary and fair. For this purpose it will have to make provision for some kind of tripartite discussion of general policy, coupled with a procedure for dealing with anomalies and exceptions.

Any such discussion must reckon with the depth and strength of widely held but ill-informed ideas about prices and incomes. There is, for example, the notion that prices can be held down by price control. In principle there is obviously some truth in this, particularly in the short run. There are times when price control has a useful contribution to make to greater stability; and at all times the Government needs some machinery for investigating complaints of excessive prices. But no amount of price control over the past five years would have done much to check inflation unless it had been taken to the point of substituting an entirely different economic system; and this goes both for statutory control and for those more ingenious proposals that would seek to prevent employers from recovering increases in their wage-bill beyond some stated limit. The Government would be wise to return as soon as possible to a system using corporation taxation and anti-monopoly legislation as a means of operating on profits rather than one that begins with price control and ends in a gigantic cost-plus operation.

Another example is the popular belief that wage-earners should benefit directly from industrial innovation, independently of any additional exertion on their part. Whatever the merits of genuine productivity bargaining, the power of workers to intercept the fruits of new technology or improved organisation without contributing materially to their introduction must simultaneously slow down economic growth and accelerate inflation. The net return on the innovation is lowered and the incentive to embark on it reduced while at the same time workers elsewhere are given fresh reasons for seeking an increase in wages by the disturbance in relative pay for unchanged jobs. If, as seems likely, the British worker is more prone than workers abroad to demand a re-negotiation of piece-rates whenever productivity is improved by technological change, we have here one very simple explanation of the slower growth and more rapid inflation characteristic of British industry. We have also a strong reason for looking with suspicion on the inclusion in any incomes policy of any special provision for productivity bargains.

The prime need is for a continuing dialogue on wage structure between the parties concerned: not between a single trade union and a single group of employers but between representatives of all the main bargaining units, both at national level and plant level (or any intermediate level at which important settlements are concluded). The aim of such a dialogue would be to agree on a basis for wage settlements that did justice to exceptional cases without giving an inflationary boost to wages generally. There are plenty of reasons why agreement will never be easy. It cannot possibly be achieved at all if the trade unions and employers' associations are unwilling to establish the necessary machinery and prefer to negotiate individual settlements one at a time.

The trade unions are in a position of special strength that is not yet matched by a corresponding recognition of responsibility to society. Full employment gives them enormous bargaining power; but since full employment also implies that employers will be able to pass on higher wage-costs in prices, the bargain is ultimately with the consumer; and this in practice means with other workers since almost 90 per cent of consumers' expenditure comes from wage and salary earners and the recipients of welfare payments of all kinds. The sooner the trade unions treat their wage claims as claims on their fellow-workers the better. It is an illusion to imagine that the claims will eventually be met out of excess profits by some small group of capitalists.

CENTRALISATION OF WAGE BARGAINS

But if this is so, then the more wage bargains can be centralised the better. The Swedish arrangement under which the central organisations of employers and employed are brought face to face in a comprehensive negotiation is a great improvement over the decentralised arrangements in Britain. It ensures that the unions must themselves co-ordinate their claims and set them in relation to one another, allowing for drift, instead of leaving the bargaining process to work itself out in a succession of independent settlements each more inflationary than the last. No doubt this is a long way off, given the reluctance of the unions to submit to the authority of any central body, including the TUC. No doubt also the inclusion of the Government in the bargaining process would raise further problems which the Swedes have not had to face. Nevertheless, if incomes policy is to work, some form of central control must be devised.

This control might be imposed from without, for example, by some pseudo-independent body, ruling on each claim or settlement submitted to it.' Taken to its limit, this might lead to compulsory arbitration; short of that, it would tend to break down as soon as rulings were challenged in a determined strike called by some major union. The alternative is to exercise control from within in the course of the bargaining process. Whatever bargain was struck—like any other collective bargain—would have to be observed by all parties. The unions would be in a position where they had to bargain not only with employers and government but with one another; and they would have to find their own methods of dealing with mavericks who refused to honour the agreement.

Centralisation in wage-bargaining will not be easy to achieve. There may be no escape from a long struggle between the Government and individual unions with the Government seeking to impose its will, the unions resisting and success alternating with failure as opinion veers this way and that, and the unions avoid confrontation or see nothing to lose by it. Such a struggle can hardly be called incomes policy. But it may be all that can be hoped for so long as the unions are unable to exercise their social responsibilities.

If we look beyond confrontation to the market forces eating away at price stability, there is a quite different programme for the

Government to mount: a programme to check drift, increase mobility and elasticity of labour supply, expand re-training facilities and allow the economic system to function with less need for periodic wage adjustments. Far more effort needs to be put into remodelling wage-systems so as to bring pay within the factory under stricter managerial control and make it less prone to anomaly and drift. Then there is the need to make better provision for the elimination of labour shortages without distorting the wage structure in the process: to upgrade, re-train and transfer workers in order to relax local pressures on manpower. At a further remove there is the need for better regional balance in the labour market and the avoidance of any wide variation in pressure between one region and another.

It is not a very dramatic programme nor one with much popular appeal. But there is no dramatic way of mastering inflation, which is the inevitable outcome of struggles over the distribution of income; struggles that are not necessarily curbed but may be aggravated by what Professor Crossley calls the more 'overt political confrontations' of incomes policy. The simple cures for inflation either won't work or work so harshly that the disease seems attractive by comparison. If we are to put an end to cost-push inflation, we will have first to unite in agreeing that it exists and what to do about it and then go on to create the institutions necessary for the purpose.

Chapter 6

Doubts about the Trend towards Floating Exchange Rates[1]

No economist has ever refused to subscribe to the view that exchange rates should from time to time be altered. If he did, he would be exposed to the retort to the lady who announced that she accepted the universe: 'Gad! she'd better!' There may be room for disagreement over the appropriate size or structure of currency areas within which such variations are in principle eliminated. There may also be some disagreement over the kind of links that ought to be established or maintained between currency areas or monetary authorities. But changes in the terms on which one currency exchanges for another are bound to occur; and that provision should be made for them is not really in question.

What *is* in question is whether and how the monetary authorities should seek to introduce some stability into exchange rates. There is at one extreme the view that there should be no official intervention of any kind, that reserves are not intended for use except in highly exceptional circumstances, and that the forces of the market are a more reliable instrument for balancing international accounts than government agencies or monetary authorities. At the other extreme is the view that depreciation should be a last resort, to be turned to after exhaustion of alternative measures. These include full exploitation of the resources of monetary and fiscal policy, with, if necessary, a partial and temporary retreat from full employment and various administrative expedients designed to improve the balance of payments and give time for speculative pressure to pass or any underlying weakness in competitive power to be overcome. Both extreme positions may be qualified, the one by accepting the need for some intervention by the monetary and fiscal authorities, the other by accepting limits to the efficacy of intervention and the need not to defer exchange rate changes too long in the face of sustained market pressures.

[1] An earlier and shorter version of this paper appeared in *Euromoney* (August 1972, p. 2). It was drafted at the Brookings Institution, Washington, D.C., to which I am deeply grateful for the opportunity of writing it. The present version was also drafted in 1972 and after minor amendments was published in *Essais en l'honneur du Professeur Jean Marchal*, Vol. I (Paris, Editions Cujas. 1975).

In the end most economists find themselves recognising the inescapability of *some* element of exchange rate management in an economy purporting to be managed and the equal inescapability of *some* responsiveness to market forces in an economy in which such forces operate relatively freely. But they do not agree on the mix; and the predominant view among professional economists does not appear to stay the same from one generation to the next. At the end of the war, in the days of the dollar shortage, the emphasis was on management and control; now, after a quarter of a century, the pendulum has swung back and there is a much greater willingness to let the rate reflect the immediate pressures of the market.

What regime is adopted must to some extent reflect the kind of world it is intended to fit. Exchange stability cannot be greater than the stability of the economies that exchange rates link together. If domestic economic management, for example, is powerless to influence the behaviour of money wages and costs, it, cannot look for greater success in controlling the external value of the currency. If private capital flows are on a scale vastly in excess of available reserves of foreign exchange, the monetary authorities may have to yield to *force majeure*. In the management of the exchanges the strategy of the authorities has to be conditioned by the weapons at their disposal and the alternative mechanisms of adjustment that they can bring into play.

There is no doubt that the world has changed greatly over the past thirty years since the discussions leading up to Bretton Woods. Governments are more at the mercy of inflationary forces and these forces leave less room for alternative strategies in adjusting to external deficits. If the pace of inflation differs widely from country to country and if this has to be accepted as a fact of life to which governments must adapt their policies, there may be no option to a system of floating rates. So long as governments have not thrown in their hands, however, it is too early to treat fixed rates as a thing of the past. Governments are still struggling to assert themselves against the drift to inflation with an increasingly keen sense of the penalties that surrender to the drift would exact.

THE LIMITATIONS OF MARKET FORCES

Let us go back to the state of thinking after the war when the dollar dominated the controversy. We had all learned from wartime experience that it was not possible to mobilise an economy for war efficiently and quickly by relying on market forces and that controls of various kinds short-circuited the desired reactions on supply and demand.

The primary reason for not relying exclusively on market forces was that, even when they worked uniformly in the right direction, it took time for the full response to manifest itself and the final outcome was not foreseeable with any certainty. Any attempt to rely entirely on market forces to bring about large and immediate changes was bound to give rise to major shifts in relative prices which might not, taken together, operate very powerfully in the direction desired and might have side-effects—particularly on the distribution of income—which would make them unsustainable or thwart the major objective. Market forces therefore tended to be used as auxiliary to the more powerful weapon of compulsion whether this was applied through rationing, licensing, conscription or in some other way.

A great deal of this reasoning still held in peacetime when post-war reconstruction began. Countries recovering from war are rarely wise to leave the adjustments entirely to market forces since the shifts to be brought about in the use of resources are on a scale and of an urgency comparable with those involved in mobilisation for war. There was also in 1945 a marked disequilibrium in the international economy between the United States on the one hand and the industrial countries of Western Europe on the other. The European countries needed time to effect the reallocation of resources involved in building up their export industries and in expanding output for civil purposes with all the additional imports that this implied, and they were doubtful whether any rate of exchange would have enabled a balance to be struck with the United States in the absence of various forms of import control. In the early post-war years, therefore, there was no strong case for leaving the exchange rate to be fixed by market forces since the domestic economy of the combatant countries remained, for good reasons, under strict control.

The devaluations of 1949 marked the end of this phase. While many countries maintained controls, and convertibility was not fully established for nearly a decade, the changes in exchange rates brought about in 1949 were intended to throw much more of the weight of adjustment to the dollar shortage onto market forces by providing fresh incentives to give preference to dollar markets and to economise on imports obtained from dollar sources. In spite of the upset of the Korean war that followed, it can be argued that the forces set in train by the devaluations in 1949 were in the end successful and laid the basis for the move to convertibility towards the end of the fifties.

All this may seem of limited relevance to exchange rate changes in the 1970s. It is true that the adjustments that any one country has to make are no longer on the scale that were called for at the end of the war and that the use of controls need no longer be contemplated and would no longer be justified by the considerations mentioned above. But the limitations of market forces of which the war provided so many illustrations still apply. That is, it takes time for the response to these forces to make itself felt and the final outcome is never exactly predictable.

The British devaluation of sterling in 1967 and the suspension of gold payments in 1971 by the United States provide clear examples of the limitations of market forces. It is easy in retrospect to point to the transformation in the balance of payments of both countries that was set in motion by the changes in exchange rates that took place. But it was a long time before there was evidence of *any* improvement and a good deal longer before the market accepted that the evidence was convincing. At the end of 1968 it should have been apparent that sterling was on the mend and that the new parity would hold.[1] Yet the following six months were perhaps the most anxious of all, and even in the middle of 1969 sterling remained weak. Had sterling been allowed to float in 1967 the rate would certainly have fallen further and there can be no equal certainty that it would have recovered. Once the anxieties of sterling holders were quickened by a continuing fall in the rate, the downward swing could have developed a powerful momentum of its own and provoked fresh irreversible inflation in the domestic market. Similarly, it took a very long time for the American balance of payments to pull round after the Smithsonian agreement and the market was slow to recognise the evidence of a change well after it had begun. The deficit had almost disappeared by the second quarter of 1973 but further devaluations of the dollar were not avoided in February and June. The possibility that the market would overestimate the fall in the rate that would prove necessary was by no means merely theoretical in the case of the dollar; and although the reaction on the US domestic economy may have been comparatively harmless, the big swing in the dollar and the fact that it was left to float contributed to the unsettlement in commodity markets in 1972–3

[1] This is not the wisdom of hindsight. I said as much at the time and left government service at the end of 1968 in the conviction that devaluation had done its work successfully.

by aggravating the underlying uncertainty in currency values and removing the lid on international prices that went with fixed rates.

There are four good reasons why any country should hesitate to abandon what powers it enjoys to keep exchange rates under control and leave them to be settled by market forces. These four reasons operate in favour of some degree of fixity in rates and justify some resort to administrative methods of buttressing an existing rate rather than leaving it to fluctuate with market pressures.

Elasticities

The case for relying on market forces is in proportion to the size of the elasticities on both sides of the market. Where these are high, it means that the process of adjustment can come about relatively easily and painlessly. But where they are low there is a risk of perverse reactions that may delay or aggravate the problem of adjustment. It is a well-known theoretical proposition that if the elasticities of demand for imports and exports do not together exceed unity the effect of a change in the exchange rate may be to add to the size of the debit balance of payments (or, where the rate is appreciated, of the surplus in the balance of payments). Even if the elasticities are considerably in excess of unity over a long period of time, they may in the short run be disappointingly low; and there is nothing in the literature to establish that over the first six months or so after a change in exchange rates, the impact on the balance of trade will be in the direction desired. Whatever calculations economists may make they cannot say with certainty *how soon* the balance of trade will begin to improve or *by how much* it will eventually be improved by a change in the rate of exchange.

These propositions still apply if one adopts an absorption approach to international adjustment. Prices may move in a direction favourable to a switch into exports and to economy in imports; but if the initial outlay on imports is greatly increased and the responses to price changes are feeble, the net effect may well be an increased rather than a diminished deficit.

Lags

The problems raised by low elasticities are greatly enhanced by what are rather gaily called 'lags in responses'. In an economy where these responses are feeble or slow (possibly for very good reasons) there may be no visible help from the movement of the exchange rate for some considerable time and the deficit may even be intensified.[1] In all problems of applied economics it is extremely important in what sequence things happen and lags have consequently an importance which is not always apparent in theoretical exposition. If the changes in prices that accompany devaluation give rise, for example, to high wage claims because of the rise in the cost of living, the immediate impact on the competitive position of the country may be substantially weakened or eventually even reversed. This point is of sufficient importance to warrant separate treatment.

Inflation

Devaluation or downward movements in exchange rates have in principle an inflationary impact on the domestic economy.[2] So far as this operates on demand, it may be contained, and to some extent offset, by an appropriate monetary and fiscal policy. But the impact on costs and prices is more difficult to control. It may indeed be aggravated by the efforts made to limit demand: for example, because higher indirect taxes raise the cost of living or because higher interest rates are reflected in a rise in rents. It is not possible to guarantee in advance that the effect on costs will be small in relation to the competitive advantage gained by devaluation. In an open economy, heavily dependent on foreign trade, imported raw materials will increase in price automatically and in a ratio that may approximate to the change in the value of the currency. This, together with the higher cost of imported food and manufactures, must increase the cost of living and this increase, after all but very small depreciations, may set off claims for higher wages. If these are conceded a fresh round of price increases is likely to follow. A succession of small changes in the exchange rate, if all in one direction, would produce the same result. Moreover, if the immediate effect on the balance of trade is perverse or, if favourable, at least not easy to identify and demonstrate, there may well be damaging

---

[1] This phenomenon is often referred to as a J-curve reaction. This description is, however, misleading since it implies that one can count in advance on a subsequent improvement without a further change (or changes) in the rate of exchange.

[2] The argument that follows is almost exclusively in terms of a falling rate of exchange. The opposite case of an appreciating rate also presents severe difficulties. The impact on the economy is in the first instance deflationary and requires changes in relative prices, including an absolute fall in the price of traded goods, that are bound to be highly unpopular politically (cf. W. S. Salant 'Intermediate Goals and Next Steps for the International Monetary System'. Brookings Institution, September 1971.)

repercussions on expectations in the market as to the future course of the exchange rate. It may be widely assumed that the downward movement has proved insufficient and that a further devaluation is called for. But if the rate reflects this pressure, the rise in import prices and the corresponding carry-through to the cost of living will be still greater so that claims for upward adjustments in money wages are likely to be all the stronger. In so far as these claims are successful, the natural consequence will be still more distrust in the capacity of the downward change in exchange rates to bring about the necessary adjustment in payments and receipts. Hence a *dégringolade* of the exchanges is not to be excluded.

Capital Movements

On top of all this we may have to take account of the flow of capital, particularly if the country devaluing is a large debtor on short-term capital account. In the case of sterling, for example, there were very large holdings within the sterling area; and it was always possible that the members of the sterling area might at some point lose their nerve and try to get out of sterling if the exchange rate began to move down alarmingly. Whatever theory may be applicable to a country whose short-term indebtedness is relatively limited, a country that is acting as an international banker is particularly at the mercy of popular opinion as to the value of its currency; and if things do not appear to be going well there may be heavy sales of the currency with all the consequences outlined above.

It may be objected that these arguments apply broadly to *any* change in exchange rates and have little or no special application to the way in which changes such as are agreed to be necessary should take place. If, for example, governments delay parity changes because of reluctance to devalue (and not because they prefer the existing rate to any other) they may avoid immediate embarrassment and difficulties of adjustment only at the cost of far greater difficulties and risks later on. The fact that it takes time for devaluation to work is surely an argument for starting early, not for putting off a decision until there is little or no room for manoeuvre. Moreover, if there can be no confidence that market forces will operate in the right direction or with the necessary force it is also possible to doubt whether administrative devices to maintain a fixed parity are likely to prove successful in the face of market scepticism.

Objections along these lines are reasonable enough. It may be right to yield to strong market pressure sooner rather than later if there is considerable uncertainty as to the appropriateness of the rate of exchange. It may be better to make a comparatively small change, in token of that uncertainty, than to run the risk of having to make a much larger move eventually from a weaker position. But it would be an illusion to suppose that there is some unique rate of exchange that is appropriate at any moment. The argument developed above implies that over quite a wide range of rates the basic balance of payments may prove remarkably insensitive for quite long periods of time and that, while a change may offer temporary relief from speculative pressure, the pressure may build up again if the effects on the basic balance are small or perverse. The domestic measures that would be necessary to defend the existing rate may be less damaging in the long run than the measures required once the rate is allowed to float.

What this comes to is that, in some countries at least, the rate of exchange is not a simple reflection of the behaviour of the domestic economy but is itself one of the principal determinants of that behaviour. The economy may dance to the tune of the rate of exchange and not *vice versa*. To the extent that this is true, control over the rate of exchange is an indispensable element in control over the economy and is not likely to be abandoned by any government seeking to exercise such control.

THE CASE IN FAVOUR OF FLOATING RATES

Let us now approach the question from the other side and ask why a government should abandon control over exchange rates. What is the logical foundation of the case for freely floating rates?

The Need for Flexibility

First of all, there is the argument that the rate of exchange is a price like any other price so that it is inherently wrong to seek to control it in a world in which prices are left to be determined by market forces. This can hardly be regarded as a very powerful argument in a society in which many prices for public services are not market-determined (health, education, defence, roads, justice, etc.) while others are regulated by publicly appointed agencies. But in any event the rate of exchange is not just a price like other prices. There are at least four important points of difference.

To begin with, the rate of exchange is more than a price: it is the basis on which the prices of all traded goods are determined. In this it resembles the price of labour (which is also not 'just a price') except that there is no single price of labour in the sense in which there is a single price (within narrow limits) for foreign exchange of all kinds. The wage structure may be relatively stable but it is nowhere near so stable as the structure of exchange rates. If the exchange rate changes, therefore, the consequences are of a quite different order from the consequences of a change in any other 'price'. The entire price structure—notably the relation between the price of non-traded goods and services (including labour services) and the price of traded goods and services—undergoes a change which affects both the direction and the level of economic activity. No other price change within the discretion of the Government (except perhaps the rate of interest) has anything like the same effect on the economic performance of the whole economy.

This implies, secondly, that the rate of exchange is an instrument of economic management in a sense to which other prices cannot lay claim. In this it resembles the rate of interest which many economists who favour floating rates would be unwilling to leave to be settled by market forces.

Given that it is an instrument of control it is also, of necessity, a political instrument. Changes in the rate of exchange affect different social groups differently and they are bound to express their interest and concern in ways that brings pressure on governments. Once it is clear that political objectives are at stake—such as the distribution of income, the cost of living, the profitability of past investments, the incentive to develop particular industries or locate new factories in particular areas—the Government cannot disengage from exchange rate management and disclaim interest in the rate of exchange, however it is determined.

Even if governments had no domestic objectives to safeguard they would be obliged to take note of the interest of other countries and governments in the price of their currency. For the price of foreign exchange is a two-sided affair; and other governments may insist on the observation of certain rules of individual behaviour in exchange markets. Fear of competitive devaluations was the basis of the Articles of Agreement of the IMF. That fear may now be less acute than before the war; but this is precisely because rates have been kept relatively stable and changes have had to be approved by the IMF. If there were a general return to floating rates, countries might be less willing to refrain from retaliation in their manipulation of exchange rates and this retaliation might soon escalate from one restriction to another, including trade restrictions of all kinds. Nor would it be sufficient for any country to say in defence of fluctuations in its rate that these only reflected market forces. If these fluctuations disturbed the basis on which production was carried on by traders in competing countries and the rate of exchange could be represented as undervalued, it would not matter whether it resulted from direct government intervention or from speculative reactions to government declarations of policy or government management of the domestic economy.

The Need for Automaticity

This brings us to the second argument for floating rates: that by relying on market forces from day to day, one escapes the political pressures that build up against necessary changes or against acting on exchange rates in good time. The issue is essentially whether it is realistic to assume that exchange rate variations can ever be free of political influences. It is an attractive but insidious argument that the struggles of the authorities to decide what to do with the exchange rate are unnecessary and that they are likely (if not practically certain) to make matters worse by their interventions. If market forces would do the job anonymously and better, then exchange rate decisions could be taken out of politics and all the spurious drama of major devaluations or revaluations would disappear.

But in fact these decisions are by their nature political. In recent years it has been the Prime Minister or President on whom the responsibility to take them has usually fallen; and it would be quite unrealistic to suppose that any self-denying ordinance which one Prime Minister took would be binding on his successors. The nearest one might get to removing decisions of this kind from politics would be the adoption of some rules of action that made parity changes mandatory in certain circumstances: for example, changes proportionate to the divergence in the market rate from the official parity over some stated period. But it is not to be expected that fully automatic rules of this kind would ever be acceptable to governments that sought to retain full discretionary powers over other instruments of policy.

The Infirmity of Governments

The main argument for letting the rate float—or indeed for any form of automaticity—is that the authorities are not smart enough and that market forces reflect underlying economic realities that the authorities may seek to ignore. This is not an argument that can be resolved by appeal to first principles since it depends ultimately on experience of both systems. But there are a number of observations that are relevant to any judgment on the matter.

First of all, it is notable that when the world last experienced a *system* of floating rates in the 1930s it was by no means enamoured of it. Most countries did not take long to peg on the pound or the dollar once they had abandoned the direct link with gold. The sterling-dollar rate itself became progressively more stable with every year that passed: not because the market by itself produced this result but because the British authorities accumulated sufficient reserves to give them confidence in their power to hold the rate steady. (They not only had the *masse de manoeuvre* which the reserves provided but the evidence provided by the trend in reserves that the balance of payments was in surplus at the current rate.) After the Tripartite Agreement of 1936 exchange rates between industrialised countries were as far from floating as they were in the twenties or fifties. The evidence of the inter-war years may bear out the view that there is nothing absurd or impossible about a world of floating rates but it also bears out the conclusion that there is something transitory and inherently unstable. 'Clean' floating for any length of time is not likely to occur.

Next, it needs to be emphasised that a quite undue proportion of the literature on floating rates seems to bear on the sterling and dollar exchange rates rather than on the rates for other currencies. An exception must be made for the German mark but there is remarkably little, except in generalised form, either about the three other currencies that one might regard as of major importance (yen, franc and lira) or about the currencies of the minor industrialised countries (kronor, guilder, Swiss franc, etc.). The less developed countries are in a special category and different arguments may well apply to them.

Yet if one had to single out the two currencies least adapted to a regime of floating rates, these two would almost certainly be the dollar and sterling. Where there are large external holdings of any currency, and where investment transactions are either of preponderant or at least major importance, it is absurd to argue as if the only question at issue was the trade balance and what might be comparatively small movements in it. Official holders of reserve currencies would tend either to dispose of them if they fluctuated at all widely (and this would for the time being intensify the swings) or else hitch the value of their own currency more tightly to the reserve currency and perhaps peg on it.

It is probably fair to say, too, that the movement of international opinion in favour of greater flexibility largely reflects a judgement on British experience in the sixties reinforced by subsequent German and American experience. Again, the special difficulties of the reserve currency countries loom very large, without much allowance for the distinguishing features of such currencies. On the British case, moreover, current professional judgements seem remarkably one-sided: it would be possible to argue that the maintenance of the rate into 1967 did very little damage to production in earlier years although the manner in which devaluation was carried out involved an expensive loss of reserves and made the subsequent adjustment process unnecessarily nerve-wracking.

We have also to take into consideration the information on which a judgement as to exchange rates is based. In a managed economy market forces divorced from the actions and declared intentions of the authorities do not exist. Those who deal in currencies have to assess, not just the competitive position of a given country (on which they might or might not reach a sound judgement) but the policies that governments are likely to pursue and the success that their policies might have in influencing the balance of payments. It is only if it is assumed that governments are not likely to have much effect on the balance of payments or if the trade balance dominates the movement of exchange rates to the virtual exclusion of capital movements, long and short, that market forces can be opposed to government operations as if the two things never interacted.

But it needs no demonstration that governments can and do influence the level of demand (and hence of trade) very considerably as well as (to a much lesser extent) the behaviour of costs and so the underlying competitive position. Moreover, governments can take action on the capital balance either through monetary policy, or various controls, or by mobilising foreign credits; and although these may be represented as temporising measures delaying an adjustment called for by a distinct trend in the trade balance, they may also, by the mere passage of time, make an adjustment less necessary or alter market opinion as to its likelihood. Nor is it to be supposed that governments will never prefer to retain controls in conjunction with an existing rate rather than move to a new rate and abandon the controls. Governments may continue as an element in the market and use their powers to push the market towards a new balance. If market opinion is a factor in its own right and an inevitable element in market forces, so also is official opinion.

These considerations have to be looked at in the light of the fundamental problem of predictability. Once a rate of exchange is allowed to fluctuate it is extremely difficult for anyone to know where it will settle; and it is much too easy to assume that speculative pressures will prove to be stabilising. Speculators are likely to take a short-term view and to be guided by the way the rate is currently moving. Indeed, they are faced with the same problem as faces the authorities when they are trying to make up their minds whether there is a 'fundamental disequilibrium' or indeed whether the existing rate of exchange calls for adjustment. At any point in time the indicators are inevitably conflicting. Those who have their eyes fixed on the behaviour of the balance of trade may react one way while those who are looking at the flow of long-term capital may react in quite the other direction. The interpretations placed on short-term movements of capital may also differ widely.

The Need for Continuous Adjustment

The final argument for floating rates to be considered is that they guarantee smaller and more frequent changes in rates and so provide automatically the greater flexibility that everyone agrees to be desirable. The system in use in the post-war period, on the other hand, involved—so it is argued—large and unsettling changes after disastrous delays.

Here we come to the crux of the matter. Is it better to change the rate frequently and err on the side of making a change unnecessarily? Should there be clear evidence of need before a move? How free should each country be to decide for itself? How much international discussion and agreement should precede a move? What criteria should govern international approval if called for? And what forms of intervention and control are legitimate or reasonable if market pressures on the rate are to be resisted?

He would be a bold man who would claim to return firm answers to all these questions and expect to carry conviction. It is in fact highly unlikely that different countries would subscribe to the same unambiguous answers or even return the same answers in different situations.

In 1973 there are very few rates of exchange where the questions really need to be asked. Most countries could probably be left to decide for themselves and let their rates float or change with whatever frequency they thought best, provided they were prepared to offer *ex post* justification in terms of actual or prospective deficits and provided not too many countries rushed to abandon fixed rates or adjust them every few months. But there are other countries that cannot be allowed such freedom because what they do determines the shape of the international monetary system.[1] The exchange rate policies of a very small group of countries—the United States, Germany, the United Kingdom, France, Japan and perhaps Italy and one or two others—are too important to their neighbours to be settled unilaterally. None of these countries is likely to be allowed by the others to let its rate float except as a temporary expedient. Whatever trust economists put in governments, there are stricter limits to the trust that the industrial countries will show in each others' exchange rate policies. They show little disposition to let their currencies appreciate freely. They might equally develop strong propensities to encourage depreciation with only the most slender justification. Since they continue to fear competitive depreciation, they are likely to insist on their right to question changes in rates of exchange and this is much easier to do under a par-value system.

It is, of course, true that some of the big industrialised countries have acted first and argued after. No doubt this will continue. It is also true that what has put most pressure on exchange rates has been a serious loss of reserves or an inordinate increase in them. That, too, may well continue. Finally, it is true that the industrialised countries as a group seem inclined to take a more experimental line on exchange rate management. This may mean that they yield more promptly to strong and continuing pressure on their reserves; but they are unlikely to do so automatically and invariably, and for reasons already given above, it would be wrong for them to surrender all discretion and treat market pressure as the fount of wisdom.

The conclusion to which all this leads is not that exchange rates should stay fixed or be changed only at long intervals or by large amounts. It is that the rate should normally be held stable within declared limits around a stated par value; that a decision to change the rate is necessarily an act of judgement forming an indispensable part of economic management; and that such a decision must balance opposing considerations. To hold the rate constant in face of evidence of actual or impending international disequilibrium may

---

[1] The argument of this paragraph is based on discussion with Michael Posner. The smaller countries can safely be allowed some latitude in weighing the international repercussions of their policies and it may not matter greatly if they sometimes disregard them. But if the larger countries are moved only by domestic economic considerations, what kind of international *system* can we hope for? A world of fixed rates in which one country elects to float is very different from a world of floating rates in which no country can by itself achieve fixity. In the latter kind of world, economic warfare would tend to spread from one area of policy to another unless governments came to some understanding about the key exchange rates and reintroduced some degree of fixity in them.

put too much faith in the power of economic and administrative measures to effect a gradual restoration of equilibrium. On the other hand, to let the rate change too easily and frequently has important disadvantages. It lets loose economic forces that may eventually work in the right direction but in the short run are liable to work in the wrong direction and have large and incalculable effects on the behaviour of the economy as a whole.

Chapter 7

International Capital Movements: the Future of the Controls[1]

The controls over international capital movements that came into existence in the early seventies were mainly designed to limit short-term flows and to operate on inflows rather than outflows. But there has also been a sustained attempt by some countries over the post-war period to limit long-term outflows. Controls for this purpose have a much longer history than controls over short-term inflows and may well have a more enduring future. The experience of the countries making use of controls over long-term outflows throws light on the reasons which are put forward to justify them and on the uses to which they may be put in future.

The two most important examples, since they are (or have been) the leading capital exporters, are the United Kingdom and the United States. The United Kingdom experimented with capital controls even before the war when it limited access to the London capital market, especially by borrowers from outside the sterling area. The existing system of control rests on the Exchange Control Act, 1947, which continued the powers exercised during the war over dealings in foreign exchange. British capital controls were originally one element in a comprehensive system of exchange control and although restrictions on current payments have ceased to apply since 1958, capital transfers remain subject to regulation. In the United States no system of exchange control existed to reinforce capital controls. American citizens (other than 'direct investors') remained free to place their funds wherever they chose. The American controls originated in the 1960s and were abandoned only in 1974. Beginning in July 1963 with the announcement of the Interest Equalization Tax, the measures taken by the US authorities evolved over the next five years to include first a voluntary programme in 1965 designed to limit banking flows and capital transfers in support of direct investment abroad and, at the beginning of 1968, a

[1] From *Capital Movements and their Control*, ed. A. K. Swoboda (Leiden/Geneva: Sijthoff/Graduate Institute of International Studies, 1975).

transformation of the voluntary restraints on direct investment into mandatory controls. It is arguable whether all of these should be brought under the heading of 'controls' since a tax represents a redirection of market forces as opposed to supercession by official regulations while voluntary restraint does not necessarily involve control. But the sequence of measures, all governed by a common objective and leading step by step towards administrative regulation of capital outflows, makes it desirable to treat them together.

The way in which British and American controls have operated is not well understood. In both cases the purpose of the controls has been not so much to limit foreign investment as to ensure that it is 'appropriately financed' (in the language of the British regulations), in the sense that the fullest possible use is made of funds raised abroad and any transfer across the exchanges is kept to a minimum. In the American case an important objective from 1963 onwards was to force Western Europe to develop its own capital market and find there the capital which it had hitherto raised in the United States. The Interest Equalization Tax did, in fact, kill off bond issues by EEC borrowers in New York as well as net investment in European equities and seems to have contributed to the rise of the Euro-bond market after 1963. As for direct investment, there is little or no evidence of any noticeable reduction in the scale of new investment abroad by American companies, whether in Europe or elsewhere. Between 1965 and 1970 the stock of US direct foreign investments grew from under $50 billion to $78 billion. Mr Cadle, the deputy director of the Office of Foreign Direct Investment, said categorically in 1969 that 'after talking to hundreds of businesses, we have no reason to believe that the US companies, using either foreign capital or US capital under their quotas, did not invest pretty much what they wanted to invest last year'. If that is true of 1969—and the figures are consistent with this judgement—it must have been at least as true of later years. What did happen, however, was a shift to foreign sources of finance.[1] US companies borrowed extensively in the Euro-bond market in support of their investment abroad and by 1972 had incurred a total external debt of over $12,000m. To the extent that this debt would have been financed from within the United States in the absence of controls this represents a substantial reduction in capital transfers across the exchanges.

[1] In the US case it is material that the controls applied only to large companies with access to the capital market. Direct investment under $2m. was freely permitted to any company although such investments had to be reported to the OFDI.

The British picture is more complicated but essentially similar The rules governing outward direct investment are not designed to prevent or restrict profitable investment projects but relate primarily to the method of financing. They do not appear to have had much effect on investment by the larger companies and even for smaller companies there is little evidence that plans for establishing facilities abroad were prevented or impeded. The main effect, as with American companies, has been on the source of finance; that is, it is foreign borrowing that has increased, not foreign investment that has fallen off. Direct investment in the non-sterling area (excluding oil) rose from £100m. per annum in the early 1960s to £300m. per annum in the early 1970s, and at the same time the parent companies increased their rate of borrowing abroad (either directly or in the form of Euro-currency) to over £200m. in 1970 and to still higher figures in 1971 and 1972.

More important in many ways has been the control over outward portfolio investment in the non-sterling area. As it operated in the 1960s this was designed to permit trading without restriction in foreign securities held in the United Kingdom while preventing additions to the existing stock out of freshly acquired foreign exchange. Portfolio transactions in non-sterling securities were segregated in the market for investment currency which commanded a premium over the official rate that at times was as high as 50 per cent. Transactions in securities by non-residents took place at the official rate of exchange except that, up to April 1967, sales of securities by foreigners were channelled through a separate 'security sterling' market.

Although these regulations did undoubtedly limit portfolio investment in the non-sterling area and caused the pool of foreign securities to diminish up to the mid 1960s the position in recent years has been dramatically transformed as a result of recourse to foreign borrowing by institutional investors in support of portfolio investment abroad. In 1972, for example, outward portfolio investment rose to the record total of £685m. and foreign borrowing in support of this expansion in the portfolio reached the extraordinary total of £715m.

Broadly speaking, therefore, the effect of British and American controls over long-term private foreign investment has been to encourage foreign borrowing in substitution for domestic sources of finance. But the attraction of foreign borrowing is bound also to depend on relative interest rates; and it is never easy to say how much would have been borrowed abroad in the absence of controls, nor how much would be paid off if the controls were removed. In the

British case, where interest rates are substantially above the corresponding rates abroad, it seems unlikely that the net effect of the controls on the movement of funds across the exchanges can now be very substantial, but when the flows inwards and outwards are so enormous it is difficult to predict what the net impact on the balance of payments would be if the controls were relaxed or withdrawn. In the American case there is rather more reason to think that the controls gave an extra thrust to foreign borrowing and induced American companies to have recourse to the Euro-bond market even when interest rates in that market were slightly above the corresponding rates in the United States. There are correspondingly stronger grounds for expecting that the removal of US controls will bring about substantial repayments of foreign debt obligations and increased use of American funds.

It may be suggested that these are only the proximate effects of British and American controls on the balance of payments and that there were other more obscure consequences because of repercussions on monetary policy, the trade balance, and so on. It would be true of most controls that one ought to look beyond their immediate impact. But it is doubtful whether this would alter the picture just given of the outcome of British and American capital controls. Any reduction in domestic borrowing in Britain or America must clearly have had repercussions on the capital market in those countries just as increased borrowing in the Euro-bond market or elsewhere had repercussions on other capital markets. But if we assume that there was no displacement of physical asset creation from one country to another because the investment would have been carried out whatever the source of the finance, the repercussions of capital controls may have been relatively unimportant. What changes they produced in interest rates and the level of economic activity depended on the action taken by the monetary authorities. If foreign central banks held fewer dollars, for example, while at the same time corporate bond issues in New York were somewhat lower, there was an opportunity for an opposite substitution of long-dated for short-dated US government debt provided those responsible for debt management wished to maintain an unchanged interest rate structure. Similarly, if European central banks found themselves with lower reserves because their nationals switched into Euro-bonds and so furnished American corporations with the liquid funds that would otherwise have been created as the counterpart of a dollar transfer, there was no particular reason for offsetting action except perhaps for some marginal reduction in reserve requirements.

The British and American controls over long-term private investment illustrate the four main purposes by which such controls are
commonly justified. These can be summarised as follows:
(i)   to influence the direction taken by inward or outward capital
      flows;
(ii) to operate on the long-term balance between domestic and
      foreign investment, e.g. in order to increase the proportion of
      domestic savings invested at home;
(iii) to reduce the pressure on the balance of payments;
(iv) to extend the freedom of manoeuvre of the monetary authorities.

I THE DIRECTION TAKEN BY CAPITAL FLOWS

Both Britain and the United States have used their controls to
discriminate between different borrowing countries. In the American
case, for example, Canada and the less developed countries enjoyed
exemption from the Interest Equalization Tax and Japan was granted
partial exemption. Similarly, countries were grouped under three
different headings for the purposes of the mandatory controls over
direct outward investment and different rules applied to each group.
In the British case a distinction was drawn from the start between the
sterling area and other countries.

These forms of discrimination were more a consequence of the
introduction of the controls than a deliberate effort to help any
particular group of countries. But once the discrimination existed
there were those who relished it for its own sake. Many of the Commonwealth countries, for example, regarded their access to the
London capital market and to British sources of capital as a kind
of *quid pro quo* for any inconveniences involved in membership of the
sterling area.

The attempt to influence the direction taken by foreign investment
is usually much more prominent, however, when control is exercised
at the receiving end. Many of the countries in which investment
takes place now seek to impose conditions on the operation of
foreign-controlled undertakings without as a rule imposing similar
conditions on foreign borrowing. The host country may wish to have
a say in the location of the plant, or in the contribution which it makes
to training skilled workers or importing new technology, or it may wish
to limit foreign participation in particular industries or even particular
enterprises. It is not necessary to elaborate on the wide variety of
capital controls of this kind. For present purposes it is sufficient to
recall that they have expanded and look like going on expanding.

II THE BALANCE BETWEEN DOMESTIC AND
FOREIGN INVESTMENT

Controls dominated by the second objective are mainly over outward flows and are usually exercised over long-term investment, whether direct or portfolio. Some of the controls exercised by continental countries limiting access to their capital market by foreign borrowers may spring in part from concern over the adequacy of domestic savings to meet domestic capital requirements. But the prime example of a country moved by considerations of this kind is the United Kingdom. In the days before 1914 when up to half the annual savings of the country were invested in foreign securities there was much controversy over what was attacked as a 'drain' of British capital. In practice nothing was done to limit foreign investment until the 1920s when it was no longer on the same scale. It will be remembered that at that time Keynes expressed concern over chronic overlending. What he chiefly had in mind was no doubt the pressure that this puts on an over-valued rate of exchange; but he was also anxious that British industry should not be starved of capital. This consideration has been prominent in later discussion of British capital controls; and it might well feature in any official exposition of the need to maintain capital controls under conditions when the pound is floating.

Fears of this kind are usually exaggerated. Industry—or at least manufacturing industry—is not the major source of demand for capital and is unlikely to be the chief victim of any increase in foreign investment. Even in the years before 1914 there is very little evidence —in spite of frequent assertions to the contrary—that investment in British industry, as distinct from housing, transport, and various forms of public investment, was depressed below the level in years of less active foreign investment. In the recent past there are even stronger grounds for arguing that so far as home and foreign investment are in competition it is public investment rather than private which interacts with foreign investment. Local authority borrowing has been a key element in the British international accounts for some time and in the past year or two public sector borrowing from abroad has been rapidly expanding. If there were evidence of a shortage of savings associated with capital outflow to sustain investment abroad it would be open to the public authorities either to borrow abroad more heavily themselves or to add to their own savings by appropriate fiscal measures. It would only be where such measures were politically difficult or economically ineffective and where there were good grounds for refraining from public sector borrowing abroad that action to prevent the diversion of savings into foreign investment was justifiable.

Such action, in any event, need not take the form of capital controls. There are other ways, such as changes in the tax system, of operating on the long-term balance between domestic and foreign investment. Indeed, from what has already been said above, it is open to doubt whether the capital controls employed by the United Kingdom now exercise much influence on the division of domestic savings between home and foreign investment. The movement of long-term funds appears to reflect the relative cost of borrowing in alternative markets much more than the restrictive influence of controls over outward investment.

III PRESSURE ON THE BALANCE
OF PAYMENTS

The controls so far discussed are not very relevant to the functioning of the international monetary system since, once imposed, they are usually maintained in the face of short-term fluctuations. It is the third and fourth objectives that are at the centre of the controversy. In the short run at least capital movements put pressure on the balance of payments; and the issue is essentially whether to try to eliminate or diminish that pressure by restricting capital movements or alternatively how, in the absence of such restrictions, equilibrium should be restored. Should the international movement of capital be checked by a change in monetary policy with all its domestic consequences? Or should the exchange rate be allowed to float in the expectation that this will procure the necessary adjustment either in the capital balance or in the current account? Should efforts be made to insulate the current account from pressures deriving from capital flows that seem likely to prove episodic and without any root in the normal structure of trade and payments?

These are questions to which each country will return its own answer, depending on:

(a) the methods of domestic economic management which it favours;

(b) the responsiveness of its current balance to the measures available to it;

(c) the international monetary system of which it forms part; and

(d) the likely impact and effectiveness of any controls that it might devise.

It is obvious, for example, that in any centrally planned economy, or even in one making extensive use of controls for purposes of domestic economic management, capital controls will be likely to prove more acceptable (and more necessary) than in economies willing to rely more heavily on market forces. By the same token, floating rates of exchange will fit better with the views and habits of the latter type of economy than with those of the former. The future of capital controls must therefore depend to some extent on the system of economic management in vogue.

The system of economic management is unlikely to be simply a matter of political ideology and must reflect to some extent what has been found to work in practice. There may, for example, be a strong aversion to floating rates in countries with large external liabilities uncovered by exchange guarantees. Or experience may suggest that the balance on current account would respond feebly or perversely to depreciation of the exchange rate. Alternatively, countries may be unwilling to run the risk of a deterioration in their terms of trade in an effort to bring their current surplus into line with a larger capital outflow. In these circumstances capital controls would find some justification in helping either to stabilise the exchange rate or to avoid less favourable terms of trade.

The choice which a country makes also depends on the international regime in respect of trade and payments within which it operates. This is partly a matter of following the prevailing fashion and partly of obeying the rules of the game, either out of regard for the common interest or because it does not pay to break them. If other countries are floating, it is impossible to have a fixed rate. If other countries have capital controls it becomes harder to avoid introducing them. A country which, left to itself, might prefer to let its exchange rate float may be less than happy when everyone else floats too and may be willing to enter into an international agreement to limit floating even if this obliges it to contemplate the imposition of capital controls. In a sense, this is the proposition that was put by the British to the American Government in the discussions leading up to Bretton Woods.

But there is also, and perhaps more importantly, the question of effectiveness. If for any reason capital controls simply do not work it would be an illusion to rely on policies which assume that they do. So far as control over long-term capital movements is concerned, there seems ample evidence that they can be made effective, although never, of course, completely so. The high premium on investment currency in the case of the United Kingdom bears this out. But not all capital controls (even over long-term investment) are particularly effective and it is as true of capital controls as of others that the more reliance has to be put on them the less effective they are.

IV FREEDOM OF MANOEUVRE OF THE
MONETARY AUTHORITIES

Where a country is willing to surrender its freedom of action in monetary policy and conform to changes in credit conditions elsewhere, it does not need to control capital flows resulting from differences in monetary conditions. At the same time, if the exchange rate is left to float (and setting aside the issues as to the terms of trade, variability of the current balance, etc. that are raised by long-term capital flows), the case for seeking to regulate pressure on the balance of payments by means of controls over short-term capital movements either disappears or coincides broadly with the case for dirty floating. As Henry Wallich has pointed out, it is difficult to have simultaneously an independent monetary policy, fixed exchanges and no control over capital movements. The more freedom of manoeuvre is sought in monetary policy and the more fluctuations in exchange rates are limited, the greater is likely to be the need for controls over capital movements. Conversely, the case for capital controls is weaker the more readily one contemplates floating exchange rates and/or abandonment of monetary weapons for domestic purposes.

It is, of course, a mistake to start from the assumption that the international mobility of capital deprives a country of all power to frame a monetary policy appropriate to its domestic needs. Even Canada, with her close attachment to the US economy and the absence of any barrier to the flow of funds, appears to retain about half the freedom of action that she might be expected to enjoy in the absence of capital movements induced by changes in interest differentials. But the greater the mobility of capital the greater the need for some form of friction or control to restrain unwanted shifts of funds between one country and another.

The discussion so far has been almost entirely about long-term investment. But over the past few years the main fluctuations have been in short-term capital flows. When the US mandatory programme was introduced in 1968 it was designed to bring about an improvement in the US balance of payments of $3b.; and in fact *in that year* although the gross outflow of private long-term capital was almost unchanged, the net flow, thanks to foreign borrowing, did improve by $4b. At no other time was the swing from year to year in the long-term flow as large. But the fluctuations in the flow of liquid funds were very much bigger. Between 1969 and 1970, for example, there was a swing of $15b. in the recorded net outflow and in 1971 a further swing in the same direction of $11b. if one adds in the enormous 'errors and omissions' item of that year. While the experience of 1968 showed that control over long-term capital movements did appear to have some effect on the balance of payments, the experience of 1971 showed that efforts to control short-term flows at the receiving end were not very effective to judge from the enormous scale on which such flows, largely unrecorded and immune from control, continued to occur.

The unusual scale of short-term capital flows has reflected the influence of two major factors in the world economy. One has been the increasing realisation that the dollar was over-valued and that it was not possible to restore a satisfactory balance at the current rate of exchange between the dollar and non-dollar worlds. Fears about the future value of the dollar dislodged some of the large holdings of liquid funds that appeared to have found a settled home and have now been transferred to other currencies without any firm basis of convenience to keep them there. As soon as the dollar appears to have fallen far enough to restore equilibrium there may well be a reverse flow into dollars that could reach proportions almost as embarrassing as the earlier outflow of dollars. But in those circumstances controls over capital inflows would have become superfluous and the issue would be one to be approached in terms of the appropriate rate for the dollar (or, in the longer run, of the establishment of a new international trading currency) rather than of controls to limit and direct the flow of capital. It seems unlikely that the US would itself introduce controls over capital inflows as a way of checking an appreciation of the dollar.

The second factor at work has been inflation, which intensifies divergences between countries in the rate of increase of costs and prices, and makes frequent changes in exchange rates inevitable. Resistance to these changes in the face of growing uncertainty about parities causes large precautionary movements of funds. Resort to capital controls to limit these movements then becomes suspect as a device to avoid necessary changes in exchange rates and may, in the end, increase the pressure by encouraging further shifts in commercial credit. The use of capital controls, in other words, does not stand much chance in an inflationary world of providing an alternative to changes in exchange rates.

These considerations throw doubt on the utility of controls over short-term capital movements in the foreseeable future. If one looks further ahead other doubts arise. If monetary integration is ever achieved in the European Economic Community there can be no place for capital controls within the Community and there might be serious difficulties about controls that were effectively on transfers into dollars and yen only. No doubt monetary integration is a long way off and unlikely to come by 1978 when the controls are due to be phased out. No doubt France will continue to want monetary integration *and* capital controls and Germany remain suspicious of *both*. But if any move is made in the direction of closer integration it would seem more logical (and more realistic) that it should take the form of prohibiting short-term capital controls than that it should be aimed at fixing exchange rates between the member countries.

While the dollar remains weak, and probably for some time thereafter, the controls can be expected to continue. Fluctuations in exchange rates involve serious inconveniences and are not necessarily self-extinguishing. The monetary authorities will be anxious to limit these fluctuations and predisposed in favour of measures such as capital controls that hold out this prospect. The mere fact of floating rates does not oblige them to refrain from intervention since 'clean' floats are not likely to be the order of the day. If it is submitted that it is an illusion to suppose that capital controls will work, central banks will reply that they are rarely completely ineffective, especially if there is no strong presumption that the exchange parity is wrong. They do to some extent limit flows of capital except when the inducements to get round them are very powerful.

When we turn back to long-term capital flows much of this argument is not very relevant. Such flows do not usually play a major part in exchange crises and efforts to control them are not usually related to temporary and intermittent pressure on the exchanges. Controls over long-term movements may not be introduced on a long-term footing since, as happened with the American controls, their removal may be promised almost as soon as they have been imposed. But such controls do not in practice come and go with balance of payments pressure and they tend to change remarkably little between one crisis and the next. If they are used to stabilise the exchange rate it is against a longer time-horizon.

In a world in which the forces making for changes in parities work fairly slowly, it is possible to withstand them by a succession of devices, of which capital controls are one, calculated to take some of the pressure off the exchange rate. The function of the controls, under those circumstances, is like the function of reserves: to buy time in which to make adjustments in the balance of payments. When time is short, the adjustments have to be faster and so more violent and, because more violent, more difficult to accomplish. Reactions that in the short-term may be perverse cease to be perverse in the longer run because elasticities grow with time. Even with floating rates, this argument applies: if it is possible to buy time, the fluctuations necessary to preserve external balance will tend to be narrower and the trend over time less steep.

The question is essentially: what controls can be made effective in such a way as to offer some immediate relief from balance of payments pressure and yet without arresting necessary adjustments? Can we identify disequilibrating capital flows and penalise them? It is difficult to be confident that we can; and yet it is difficult to imagine governments declining to use controls on the grounds that they might make a mistake or fail to devise penalties.

So the issue becomes one of what kind of controls to retain and what to abandon. Control over short-term flows, except through limitations on the net position of banks in foreign assets and liabilities, is likely to diminish for reasons already discussed. Control over private outward direct investment has been of limited value and should probably be abandoned.

The trend in Britain has been to leave less and less to administrative discretion and avoid difficult judgements of priority between different projects. In the United States control has been confined throughout to the large corporations. In neither country has the scale of foreign investment, as distinct from the use made of foreign borrowing, been much affected. This is not very surprising given the dynamic character of most investment, which complicates and limits the power of outside agencies to supervise it. A very high proportion of direct investment overseas—in the British case up to 80 per cent in some years—comes from reinvested profits and it is chiefly these that sustain the rhythm and momentum of expansion. But they are not easily controlled by governments, especially when there is strong local participation in the foreign affiliate. It is much easier to insist on supplementation of reinvested profits out of new capital raised abroad rather than transferred across the exchanges; and this is the form that control has taken in the recent past. Whether it is worth continuing is doubtful, especially in the British case where foreign borrowing is cheaper and needs no special encouragement while all restrictions on direct investment in the EEC are in any event due to be wound up by the end of 1974. If they are—and it is a big 'if'—they could hardly be retained in relation to other countries. Moreover, it would seem much simpler and at least as effective to let any discouragement of outward direct investment take the form of higher taxation than make use of a quite separate, and not always easily understood, administrative control.

Control over outward portfolio investment is another matter. Here there is no complex problem of priority between applications. It is possible to segregate the market in foreign securities and allow transactions within the market in all freedom, but at a premium in foreign exchange. The central bank could intervene if it chose in order to widen or narrow the margin between the premium rate and the official rate (as happens now in the Belgian dual exchange market but not in the British investment currency market). In this way what might prove a large disequilibrating flow could be kept under control or entirely eliminated. Moreover, this form of control, although due to come to an end in 1978, could justifiably be retained within the Community even if dual exchange markets *á la Belge* had been ruled out or if direct investment by one member country in another was free from control.

It is also arguable that a control of this kind is to be preferred to the kind of tax used by the United States—the Interest Equalization Tax—to check outward flows of portfolio capital. It would not bite nearly so severely on US purchases of foreign equities and might open up again the possibility of borrowing by Western European countries in New York. Without knowing what premium would be established it is impossible to predict what changes in the US capital balance would occur if a change were made. But just as it might have been better to use a different tax on the profits of foreign investment rather than control over outward direct investment, so it might have been better not to use a tax on purchases of foreign securities and instituted a dual market instead.

Whatever form of control over long-term flows is retained, it would be a mistake to set much store by it except as a form of supplementary reserve. Capital controls, except for control over outward portfolio movements, are usually of limited effectiveness. They are neither as useful nor as damaging as arguments conducted in terms of general principle tend to assume but in an unstable world are likely to have a longer life than their intrinsic merits would justify.

Index of Names

Index of Subjects

For Product Safety Concerns and Information please contact our
EU representative GPSR@taylorandfrancis.com Taylor & Francis
Verlag GmbH, Kaufingerstraße 24, 80331 München, Germany